In the midst of *Acts of God*, you need someone to stand with you who has a heart after God. There are few I'd trust my hurting heart to more than Bob Russell. Profoundly wise, deeply biblical, and always gentle, Bob Russell is a man who writes with a heart of a pastor—and the healing love of his Savior.

ANN VOSKAMP
Author of the *New York Times* bestseller *One Thousand Gifts*

Bob Russell has a unique way of illustrating how biblical truth intersects with human need. In *Acts of God*, Bob shows how God's hand was at work throughout the life of Joseph amid the prideful immaturity and alluring enticements of youth, the pain of rejection and unjust suffering, the subtle temptations of power and success, and the sobering realities of aging and preparing for death. I will use this book as a reference for my own teaching and preaching, and I will recommend it to others who face painful situations that make them wonder about the goodness of God.

DR. DAVID FAUST
President, Cincinnati Christian University
Author, *Married for Good*

Life and business throw us some high hard ones. Bob Russell brings a commonsense perspective on how to persevere and even triumph in the toughest trials. Every successful business has a plan and this book will help us all understand God has a master plan for our lives.

DAVID NOVAK,
CEO of YUM! and author of *Taking People with You*

ACTS OF GOD
WHY DOES GOD ALLOW SO MUCH PAIN?

BOB RUSSELL
WITH ROB SUGGS

MOODY PUBLISHERS

CHICAGO

*This book is dedicated to
the memory of Pastor Gerald Comp,
whose untimely passing at age thirty-eight
was deeply painful to all who loved him.*

CONTENTS

FOREWORD

ONE OF THE FIRST funerals I ever performed for was for a young man just twenty-five years old. I say "young man," but at that time I was only twenty-one myself. I had never met him and the only thing I really knew about him was how he died—from a drug overdose.

I met with his mother to plan the funeral service. She was a single mom who had just lost her only child. She was a committed Christian but was angry with God—how could he let something like this happen?

Fresh out of seminary, I had actually written a lengthy paper for my hermeneutics class titled "Where Is God When Life Is Hard?" I began to address her problem of pain by making my way through some theological talking points. It didn't take long for her to grow tired of my words and through her tears, anger, and frustration she responded: "What does God know about—"

Then she caught herself.

I can't be certain, but I'm pretty sure she was going to finish her question with: ". . . losing a son?"

Neither of us said anything for a little while.

It may be easy to offer glib answers about suffering when others are going through it, but if you are the one who has been diagnosed, if you are the one whose marriage is falling apart, if you are the one whose job has been eliminated, if you are the one who's gotten hurt in an accident, then you know you need more than textbook answers. You need to know that God knows—and that he can be trusted.

In this much-needed book, Bob Russell helps us see more clearly the goodness of God in everyday life and how God is at work when life gets hard. Bob gives us a much-needed biblical perspective when we find ourselves asking life's most difficult questions—questions about pain and suffering that at some point every one of us will ask.

Why is this happening to me?
When will God finally answer my prayer?
What possible good can come from this?
How can I get through this?
Where is God?

More than any other pastor or author that I'm aware of, Bob Russell has a gift for addressing these questions in way that not only speaks to the head but also to the heart. He has spent decades not just studying what the Bible says about suffering but being with people going through pain and loss. Over the years, I have been with Bob as he has visited families in hospital rooms and funeral homes. I have prayed alongside him that healing would come to a young mother diagnosed with cancer. I have listened to him offer words of peace to parents who lost a child. I have been on my knees with him as we have asked for God's help. Many times I have sat in funerals and listened to Bob offer words of comfort and hope. He taught me that when you speak to those who are suffering you do so with a tear in your eye and a lump in your throat.

This is not an easy book to read. Instead of addressing this subject by wrapping up some trite talking points and sticking a bow on top, Bob deals with these difficult questions in a way that is honest and raw. You may see yourself in some of the stories. You will learn from Bob's guiding you through the story of Joseph, who knew both great success and great sorrow. Most important, you will draw closer to the heart of God.

KYLE IDLEMAN
Teaching Pastor, Southeast Christian Church
Louisville, Kentucky

1: WHY, GOD?

How to Face Life's Toughest Question

SOONER OR LATER, you'll come to it, just like the rest of us.

Sooner or later, you're going to face that moment. It's on its way, no matter who you are or how you think. The Question is in your future. You'll run right into it, head-on, in some moment of emotional turmoil.

Why, God? Why did you let that happen?

It's as much of a cry as a question, really; a wound; a shout of betrayal of all the rules of life and fairness as you knew them.

So it may be a cry, but it expresses itself, every single time, as a question: *Why?* And it expresses itself, invariably, to one person. *Why, God?*

It comes when you're facing something that doesn't fit into the picture—something terribly, frightfully wrong in every way. And it's the most basic reflex of human nature to want to know the reason.

Perhaps the worst of the moment is knowing, with some awful inner assurance, that no answer is forthcoming—at least not the kind of answer you crave. Not the full and satisfying answer your heart cries out for. In this of all moments, the heavens fall silent. Count on it.

When will you face that question? Or could it be that this is old news, that you've faced the question before. Once. Twice. Maybe more times than you can count. Maybe your mind is full of this question during this season of your life, and it's the very reason you picked up this book.

Perhaps it came when you confronted the death of a child. Perhaps it was the news of a natural disaster; perhaps some cruel, very personal heartbreak that brought the Question to the forefront of your mind.

You held it there, turned it around, and examined it from every angle, really grasping its implications for the first time—but not the last.

For, like some monster from a B-movie, the Question never dies. No matter how many times you knock it down, it always rises from the dust. There's always a sequel.

It can't be fought off, rationalized away, or overcome by the quantity and kindness of friends. There's no stake to hammer through its heart. The Question is no respecter of persons. You could be the richest person in the world, and still it is relentless, threatening that place in your soul where life makes sense, where all endings are happy ones.

Why, God? Why did this happen?
Why didn't you stop it?
Why won't you explain yourself?

Actually, the Question would never occur to us if the world weren't, overall, such a lovely place. Have you ever thought about that? Weeds aren't ugly unless they're seen in a garden or a beautiful lawn.

Our world is a garden. It's filled with majestic vistas that speak of a divine artist. We see the power of God in a sunset, feel his affection in the warmth of a little child, sense his wisdom and guidance in the cycles of life and nature. This earth is a museum of his magnificence, and we walk through it day by day, letting it fill our hearts to overflowing—until, once again, some horrendous event crashes into our midst, taunting our faith and defying our easy answers.

It's the number one question that people bring to me. *Why?* Why death, disaster, injustice on micro and macro scales? How can these things coexist with the loving, perfect God I've told them about so many times?

I tell them he is love. I tell them we are his precious, beloved children, and that he has proven it; that he paid the highest of prices to bring us home to him. I tell them he's sovereign, which means that he's got the whole world in his hands.

Their response: "Pardon us, but—*this* world? This world of tsunamis and falling towers and poisoned skies, of death and war and disease? This world in which some of us are losing our homes because we can't find work? He may have the whole world in his hands, but is there not blood on those hands?"

I tell them God identifies with their grief. They tell me, "We don't want identification; we want intervention."

They can and do believe in the God I serve. But they want to know *why*. *Why* won't he step in when life turns inside out?

Can't he?

Or won't he?

I've had a lot of years to think about these things.

✦ ✦ ✦

I'll never forget my first truly devastating experience with the Question.

It was the afternoon of homecoming at my home church, the happiest of happy days in congregational life. Homecoming is a great reunion, a joining of church present with church past. The prodigals return, and the pews are full. The aromas of home cooking drift through the building.

I was in my mid-twenties then, back for a visit; I was preaching at another church on most Sundays. It felt good to be home. We'd had a joyful worship service that morning, and people sang the hymns with gusto, though their voices were mingled with the rumblings of their stomachs. Incredible feats of cooking awaited, and everyone knew it.

It was a lovely day outdoors. We ate, we laughed, we played, and we swapped old church memories. The sounds of children's shouts rang through the air. Then those shouts—well, their tone changed. They became screams.

We came running and discovered the ghastly news. Our preacher, Gerald Comp, had dived deep into the frigid swimming hole while playing tag with some of the kids. One of the kids wanted to know why he didn't come up.

Life simply *stopped*. It felt that way to everyone. One moment, there had been laughter and play, the next it was as if death had stolen in, easily overcoming the sum of our joy.

NEVER before that moment had I ever seen my father cry.

Even now, I can close my eyes and recall the image of Gerald's wife, Barbara, and their two teenage daughters, standing with pale faces as his lifeless body was pulled from the waters. Some wept, some prayed, but most of us did both. We fell to our knees and pled with God, passionately, desperately, to glorify his name through the healing of Gerald Comp.

A group of men went about the business of resuscitation. It all came to nothing. There was our pastor, our man of God, a lifeless shell. He was having his own homecoming, death's mockery of our church's day.

Never before that moment had I ever seen my father cry.

Why, God? Why Gerald? Why our church? Were our prayers not sincere enough? Were our tears not wet enough?

Gerald Comp was a thirty-eight-year-old man, a revered pastor, a model husband and father, and a spiritual leader abounding in fruitfulness. If God wanted to remove one of his most effective servants from the earth, well, he'd certainly done that. How could there even be a reason?

From Gerald's very mouth we had heard sermons on Romans 8:28, telling us that all things work together for the good of those who love God and are called according to his purpose. Many of us could rattle the words off our tongues without thinking. But now those words had real weight; now they had implications. The apostle Paul's math seemed like an imbalanced equation—theology that didn't add up.

As the ambulance came, and the rest of us stood huddled in one another's arms, we whispered about what came next. The name *Greg* was among those whispers. *Who will tell Greg?*

Greg Comp, the pastor's fourteen-year-old son, was home with the flu; he could have no idea that his life had changed forever, that in some mundane moment, he had lost something that could never be replaced.

Someone had to go and bring the news to Greg.

Thirty minutes later, a friend and I were heading for the Comp home. I couldn't imagine what I was going to say or do, how I was going to be the harshest messenger of his life.

I was no more than a decade older than Greg. I thought about my own father, and tried to imagine myself in this position. Where would I be now if *I* had been deprived of my dad at fourteen years old? What might my life be like?

As I realized the struggles in store for Greg Comp, I felt so many things: speechless, confused, spiritually disarmed, upset. What words could I possibly say that would not come across as unfeeling platitudes?

In the end, I think I realized that any words I chose, other than the information I bore, were next to irrelevant. Most of the point was simply to be there, to share an unthinkable moment. There were no magic expressions or potions to dull his pain.

And yes, I asked it, within myself: *Where were you, God? Why did you let this happen? How is this family supposed to bear up?*

And from heaven came a profound silence—or so it seemed to me. *Why, God?*

THE USUAL SUSPECTS

Let's be honest: This is no easy question, the relationship of God to human suffering. The wise and the devout have grappled with it throughout history, and not always to a victorious conclusion. St. Teresa of Avila said, "Lord, if this is the way you treat your friends, it's no wonder you don't have many!" At least hers was less an expression of doubt than of frustration.

Others have taken hold of the Question as a kind of checkmate in the game of rationalizing God out of existence—or at least diminishing our view of him. Their line goes like this:

- God is purportedly good. Yet there is great human suffering.
- Since God doesn't intervene, he lacks either the will or the power.
- If he lacks the will, he isn't good after all. (If he's God, he isn't good.)
- If he lacks the power, he isn't God after all. (If he's good, he isn't God.)

It's a striking line of reasoning. But it's also a little too cut and dried, right? God, the world, and suffering: These are not simple issues. We all sense that there could be other reasons God would hold back from stopping anything and everything unpleasant in this world.

So we look for other reasons that evil and suffering may exist; we round up the usual suspects.

1. Discipline

Maybe it's simple cause and effect. This is the "you had it coming" argument. Once Jesus came across a blind man, and his disciples immediately asked, "Who sinned, this man or his parents, that he was born blind?" (John 9:2).

They are hoping, of course, for a lively philosophical debate with Jesus the teacher. They have been taught that disease or disability is mark of someone's sin. So whose?

Jesus tells his disciples they're asking the wrong question. It's not about who sinned, but how the goodness of God can shine through the situation. And he proceeds to make that happen. As always, Jesus gets to the root of the subject in a startling way. He shows us an old question from a brand-new angle. As we'll see, he has hit upon a key element of the problem of suffering.

We'd like to scoff at the disciples' thinking and say that our God doesn't work that way, punishing sin with suffering. The problem is, the Bible says that he does—sometimes. Moses wasn't allowed to enter the Promised Land because of a certain incident in which he lost his temper and usurped God's glory, a serious offense. Miriam, his sister, was temporarily struck with leprosy for undermining Moses' leadership.

And those are not isolated incidents. There's an important passage in Hebrews 12. It tells us that God disciplines us as a father disciplines his children—for our good. Discipline is simply a part of loving training. We do need to distinguish punishment from discipline. The former is simply a penalty dealt out for a misdeed; the latter is a loving form of training. We impose discipline on ourselves not as punishment but to be better people.

So God disciplines. But there are other angles, too.

2. Poor Decisions

Sometimes we suffer due to our own willful error. Maybe the warning was on the label all along, and we simply ignored it. The sign said the road was slippery, and we pushed the accelerator down.

> **WE** can't rail against God when we're given fair warning.

Let's say Uncle Bob's bad report from the doctor concerned lung cancer. He smoked for years, everyone nagged him about it, and he really did mean to stop. But the fact is, he didn't. He foolishly ignored the warning signs. So it's not as if God is suddenly, arbitrarily inflicting this bad medical report like a lightning bolt of sheer wrath. Uncle Bob quite sadly brought this upon himself.

Sometimes we choose the wrong friends, eat the wrong foods, make the wrong decisions in business or in family. The old TV detective Baretta used to say, "Don't do the crime if you can't do the time."

But the Bible puts it better: "Be sure that your sin will find you out" (Numbers 32:23). Life comes with any number of hazard labels. We can't rail against God when we're given fair warning. Actions have consequences.

3. Satanic Attack

Could it be the devil?

It's the simplest and most logical of arguments, in a way: All good things come from heaven, all bad things are the work of Satan. The Bible describes how he attacked a good man named Job, who suffered deeply and thoroughly.

Paul spoke of a "thorn in the flesh," some unpleasant infirmity that God allowed Satan to use as a weapon against the apostle. From the devil's perspective, it was an attack; from God's, it was a tool to protect Paul's humility.

Again, here's a compelling clue to how God relates to our pain. An attack could originate from hell, while shaping us for heaven. The devil himself—as much as he hates it—finds his own place in the vast plan of God, who is all-powerful, capable of using any element as part of the great tapestry he is knitting together.

4. The Sins of Others

The disciples suggested that the blind man may have been blind because of his parents' sins. This was logical, from their perspective, because the man had been born with his infirmity; it couldn't be his fault if he was born that way.

Sometimes relatively innocent people suffer out of all proportion to any argument of sin being the cause. A little child dies. A drunk driver steals the life of a promising young lady. An emotionally disturbed man opens fire in a theater or a school. A child is born with a drug addiction stemming from the mother's use of cocaine.

Surely God is not dispensing "discipline" through such horrendous events; it would be mere punishment, serving no purpose for the victim. No, in these cases, people are clearly suffering for the sin of others. It's an unavoidable conclusion, but not a very pleasing one: We may suffer as the consequence of others' sins.

It brings us right back to the question of God's place in this: Why would he allow the innocent to be victimized for someone else's wrongs?

And yet we read in the Old Testament the idea that the sins of the fathers are visited on the third and fourth generations. It may not seem fair, but it's the way the world turns. We must take into account that our sins put out ripples, in the world around us and the future ahead of us.

5. Persecution

Here is another striking idea from the Bible: "Everyone who wants to live a godly life in Christ Jesus will be persecuted" (2 Timothy 3:12). So maybe, bad things happen to good people *because* they're good people.

Again, this checks out logically. We know that if we take a stand for biblical values in an anti-biblical world, we will face certain consequences: ridicule, rejection, possibly loss of work or even freedom, in some circumstances. People are still punished or even executed for their faith in some parts of the world. We've seen businesses lose income when their prominently Christian leaders stood firm for biblical values. Jesus said this would happen, and there's never been a time when he wasn't proven correct.

6. A Fallen World

There's also the distinctly Christian idea that we live not just among fallen people, but in an entire fallen world. In other words, the rebellious sin of Adam and Eve caused all of creation to be corrupted. Paul teaches, in Romans 8, that all of this world "groans" as in childbirth pains, awaiting the birth of a new creation.

This helps us to account for natural calamities: tsunamis, earthquakes, diseases, floods, and even the attacks of vicious animals. We can suffer through non-human agency, and the Bible teaches us that even in these cases, we are feeling the consequences of a world that has rebelled.

As a matter of fact, we find this subject arising much more frequently in recent days. Monster storms have devastated New Orleans and New York; and even near my home, an F4 tornado twisted its way through the community at 170 miles per hour, killing eleven people and doing untold damage. These are the times when people come to me with haunted eyes and ask, "Why?"

The answer is that our planet and our people suffer from the fall of humanity. For this life, we will see the result of rebellion against God again and again, and we call the natural disasters "Acts of God."

Even so, I suspect Jesus would point out that we're still asking the wrong questions. We're quick to brand horrendous things as acts of God, but what about all things bright and beautiful? What about a gentle spring rain, a day of glorious weather, a field of ripe corn? Are these not also acts of God?

In the same way, we look to the heavens in the midst of a bad day and say, "Why me, Lord?" Bad moments are quickly dubbed "God moments." But when something good happens, we tend not to see it in that way. Fathers don't tend to hold a first newborn child, look to heaven, and cry out, "Why me, Lord? Why do I deserve such a beautiful blessing?"

When was the last time you rose in the morning and asked God why he gave you another precious day of life? Three square meals? Family, church, health?

Maybe that's one of the right questions.

WHAT EXACTLY IS EVIL?

Everyone knows that some believe God doesn't exist. You might be surprised to know that some don't believe evil "exists"! How can that be?

Augustine, the early Christian leader, believed that evil does not exist as a created entity, but as a corruption of the good that God created. Satan, he argued, cannot create at all—only God can do that. So the devil is limited to twisting good things into bad ones. For example, lust is a warped version of proper desire.

Through this argument, Augustine was one of the first thinkers to explain why God allows suffering. God is infinitely good, and nothing evil can come from him. What we call evil is the result of the free will of people, whose disobedience warps God's wonderful creation.

The entire world is impacted by the rebellion of Adam and Eve (and the rest of us, each day) as a consequence of the free will God gave us to choose—and the way we dishonor that gift. Thus we have evil, human and "natural."

Evil is never an act of God, but the result of the acts of men and women (even if indirectly so).

THE QUESTION REMAINS

We can name all these *sources* of suffering and more, but none of them get to the root of the *why* question. Wherever the bad things came from—why didn't God do something about them?

After all, we're told that God has loved us with an everlasting love. The Bible goes into incredible detail to show us the depth of that love; the fact that he has loved us as his very children, that we are God's handiwork, created by him to do good works.

Meanwhile, we're also told that God is infinitely powerful, that nothing is impossible with him. He is *sovereign*, which means that the buck stops here; he created everything, he knows when the smallest bird falls from a tree, and his hand utterly controls human destiny.

So how do we put these two realities together? How can God be both wonderfully good and ultimately powerful, while allowing all the evil that we see and experience?

> **EACH** one of us, if we intend to be serious about pursuing God, must wrestle through the night with the mysteries of good and evil.

Like everyone else, I wish God would phone me and clue me in. I know all the big theological issues, but I get frustrated; I long for him to just give me the short answer. I almost wish he wouldn't trust me so much to handle the hard questions of faith—but that's exactly what he does.

When I was in school, my mathematics text sometimes had the answers in the back of the book. I knew that no matter how difficult any problem seemed, no matter how inside out it twisted my mind, there was a wonderfully logical, perfectly neat answer on the final pages of that book.

I do believe the Bible has the answers. The "back" of the book, known as the New Testament, has the solution to every problem. But these are not encapsulated in simple numbers or a few words. They must be worked out within the human heart, and held together by the glue of faith.

I think I realized this even as my friend and I took that nightmare ride to the Comp home to tell a fourteen-year-old boy about the death of his father. I knew I'd be grappling with that *why* as long as I drew breath, and no matter how deep my faith grew. I knew that as I grew ever closer to God, my questions would only add up. Far greater minds than mine had done battle with these things. Why should I even jump into the ring?

Except that I knew I must. Just as *you* must. Each one of us, if we intend to be serious about pursuing God, must wrestle through the night with the mysteries of good and evil. Jacob did that in Genesis 32. At a crossroad moment of his life, a dark night of his soul, he was visited by a messenger of God. The two of them literally wrestled until sunset.

Jacob fought for all he was worth, and wouldn't let go until he had his blessing. Neither should we. I believe we are blessed by the courage we show when we squarely face our doubts. Conversely, we are diminished by looking the other way, closing our minds, and "protecting" our faith as if it were some weak and fragile thing.

The way to strengthen faith is to walk forward in it, facing all the hard questions and trusting in the goodness of God for resolution. I've tried to do that as long as I've known Christ, and here is what I've found: The mysteries, to some extent, endure. God must be God, and can't be reduced to the easy and rational and comfortable.

We can't make him smaller and easier to carry around in our minds; instead, our own minds and spirits must expand. They must grow stronger and wider, so that they can allow for the things that must be taken on faith. As we walk forward in that way, we do find out just how good, *and* how powerful, God really is.

As a matter of fact, I find that this is even true of people. They too are mysterious in many ways. Every ordinary person you know is a unique creation, filled with surprises and impossible to pigeonhole— the living sum total of a life no one else has lived, a uniqueness no one but God could have designed. Should we expect to understand every little thing about the Creator himself, when his people are so wonderfully unpredictable?

So God wants me to know him; he even wants me to have intimacy with him. But he doesn't want me to live under the illusion that I can get him all figured out—he would then be less than God. What he wants is for us to accept his mystery and trust his character. As I've sought to do that, I've discovered that the other questions often reveal their answers in startling and wonderful ways.

Take the story of Greg Comp, who lost his father.

THE TRUTH ABOUT SEEDS

As members and friends of the church, we stood with broken hearts as our pastor's lifeless body lay there in the grass. God could not have seemed more absent to us—his heart colder than the waters that had stolen breath from our spiritual leader. But was God truly absent, or did our tears simply blind us from seeing him? Was his heart truly too cold, or was it too deep for us to fathom the plans that he had?

I sat and talked with Greg, and saw the shock roll across him, slowly preparing him to take on the long siege of grief that would follow. Our church, too, had a period of mourning. As a matter of fact, a strange thing transpired through our sadness: Our relationships deepened. We learned to depend upon each other, to minister to each other through our personal gifts, in ways that frankly wouldn't have come about otherwise. Most of the people ultimately turned from their anger at God, simply because they needed the comfort only he could offer. They went deeper with him not in spite of their pain, but because of it. And they went deeper in their fellowship together as his children.

The day came when we reflected on our little group, no more than 150 members, and realized that we had somehow produced dozens of preachers, missionaries, and powerful servants of Christ, each of whom impacted larger circles of humanity for the sake of God's kingdom. Among those servants is Greg Comp, who at one time would pastor the same church in which his dad spent his final days. To the world at large, that would seem more than peculiar. Greg would be expected to get as far away as he could from such a tragic place that dealt him such a blow; many would predict him to walk away from God himself.

Greg sees it differently. He is his father's last and most significant gift. Gerald's life was too short, but his legacy is deep and wide and full and nowhere close to its conclusion.

That's how God does things. If you come to be a member of Greg's church, and you experience some kind of emotional turmoil, Greg can minister to you with a power and sensitivity only available to those who have known what it is to suffer, to ask the questions, and to grow in the faith even when the answers didn't come easily.

Jesus liked word pictures in his teaching, and one of his favorite visual images was the simple idea of a seed. He said the following: "Unless a kernel of wheat falls to the ground and dies, it remains only a single seed. But if it dies, it produces many seeds" (John 12:24).

Ordinary human bitterness would see the death of Gerald Comp only for the pain it brought. Trust in God sees Gerald as a seed—for that's what we all are in God's spiritual economy, seeds capable of eternal harvesting. Gerald fell to the ground, his life and devotion took root, and through him God has produced a bounty that will only be fully measured when we reunite in heaven.

> **IT'S ONE** thing to possess an eternal mindset while hearing a sermon or reading this book. But can you do that when the darkness falls?

And on that great day, I imagine Gerald will laugh with us and shake his head in awe over the wisdom and ultimate goodness of God. And he wouldn't change a thing. Gerald, of course, would have a heavenly perspective that, from his position, would make all things beautifully clear.

One of the deepest secrets of life is to be able to view reality through that kind of lens that now—to see earth through eternal eyes. "We fix our eyes not on what is seen, but on what is unseen" (2 Corinthians 4:18). Can you do that? It's one thing to possess an eternal mindset while hearing a sermon or reading this book. But can you do that when the darkness falls?

Matt Davidson was a gifted and godly worship leader in our church. During his mid-thirties, as the father of three children, he was taken suddenly and unexpectedly by an aneurysm. Again, an entire church was devastated.

Two of Matt's fellow ministers stood outside his room as the family wept and prayed by Matt's lifeless body in the hospital bed. One of them, Kurt Saunder, said to Greg Allen, the other one, "You and I believe all things are possible with God. What do you think? Should we go in and pray for God to raise Matt from the dead? Because he is all-powerful—he can do it. What a victory that would be!"

It eventually hit those two pastors that their request for resurrection would have been a very selfish one. Matt was in heaven! Why would he want to come back? If they could have spoken with Matt at that very moment and said, "Matt, we're praying for you to come back to earth," they were confident he would have responded, "Are you kidding me? Don't do that! I'm in heaven, man! I have never been so happy, I'm in the presence of Jesus. I've never felt this good. Sorry, I'll stay here and wait for you!"

THE POWER OF MINDSET

For most people today, those two preachers' conclusions would seem like an upside-down way to think about losing a close friend. It's because most people have minds attuned only to earthly things. The more we live that way, the more we come to believe this world is all there is. Eternal thinking liberates us from the desperation of that idea; it constantly refreshes us with the understanding that there is a better life, one with no more tears, no more suffering—one where we finally see Christ face-to-face.

Now, does that mean we smile and laugh when we lose someone? Of course not! Our grief is as real and as strong as the truth that we are separated, for now, from those we love. But genuine faith brings remarkable power in these situations. Our tears are tempered by the quiet joy of knowing someone we love faces no more pain, and is waiting for a reunion that we'll someday enjoy.

This book is about learning to think about the hardest question with godly wisdom. You and I face many questions, many trials. But we can face them together. Through the topics we'll approach here, we have an opportunity to focus on the practical realities of living in a fallen and hurtful world. Here are some of the issues we will explore:

- Much of the pain today is rooted in hurting families, in which children needlessly suffer. How can we take on that problem?
- What about the endless temptations we face? What happens when we're falsely accused? Again we ask: *Why must I go through these things, Lord?* And I believe there are answers and strategies for us to discuss.
- What about long periods of discouragement? Why would God have us suffer through these, and what can we do to change things? We'll talk about it.
- Conversely, what about those times when life goes well? These are the occasions when it would never occur to us to ask, *Why, God?* And therein lies the danger. The devil can be very effective in his disguise as an angel of light.
- Then there are times when others attack us. We expect people to be held accountable for their wrong actions, yet it doesn't happen. Why?
- Finally, let's return to the area of grief. These are the occasions when we ask God the hardest questions. Why must

we lose the ones we love? Why must the separation be so lengthy and painful? There are many questions here, as well as many wise approaches to the grief we all must face.

For better or for worse, we think of all these tough times as "acts of God." Maybe that's unfair of us. Yet those three words are a good start. Every time you hit a rough spot in life, you'll find it can become a true act of God, a staging area for him to do something incredible—something that grabs the attention of a world that craves answers.

When the darkness comes, we simply have to learn the art of night vision. We must see the outlines of God's hand, acting for our benefit out of his infinite love and wisdom. A man named Joseph once did that. In the pitch-black of a dungeon, he held on to the light of God's goodness, which can't be shut out no matter how deep the pit we've entered.

We'll use Joseph as our focal point for these lessons, because his struggles are so human, so recognizable, and because they give us invaluable clues to the acts of God in the midst of the struggles of people. Joseph's story is found in the book of Genesis.

But in the end, this is a book not about Joseph but about *you*. Each of the challenges noted above is one you've either faced or will face. Each represents a defining moment in your identity as a human being. Will it finally be revealed as an act of God, a cross that gives way to a crown? Your choices will make the difference.

For now, we have some unfinished business with life's toughest question. Let's discover some practical strategies for facing the *Why* by asking a better question: *How?* How can we take these trials and see them through to triumphs? In the next chapter, we'll discover some keys.

QUESTIONS FOR YOU

1. Describe the occasion when you first questioned God's goodness. What happened? How did your friends or family

view the incident? How was your view of God affected?

2. Several causes of evil are discussed. Which have been most common in your life? Which do you feel are the most difficult to deal with?

3. In an encounter with a blind man, Jesus showed the disciples they were asking the wrong question. Explain his point. How can this insight help us deal with our suffering?

4. What are some practical ways we can develop an eternal mindset, viewing our experiences in terms of God's eternal purposes?

2: NIGHT VISION

Finding Light When All Seems Dark

MOM AND DAD SMILE as they watch their son from a window. He's furiously pedaling his bike up the street, as Nubs the dog runs along, barking joyfully.

"Are you sure we're not rushing things?" asks Mom. "Seems like only yesterday he was on his tricycle. He's perfectly happy with the training wheels."

"Sure, but most of his friends have already moved on to the bigger bikes. Haven't you noticed? There's a reason they call them training wheels. They're only meant to be temporary."

"I know. I just don't want him to be afraid—and what if he falls and hurts himself?"

Dad laughs. "Has it really been so long since you and I rode bikes? He's going to fall sometime, unless of course you want to run along beside him every minute with your arms wrapped around him. You want to do that?"

"Don't give me a hard time, honey!" she laughs. "It's just that he's my baby . . ."

"Mine, too. Mine, too. But he can't be one forever."

Just before dinner, Dad gets his toolbox and calls the boy to him. "Want to help your dad with a project?" he asks. The boy's face lights up—until he sees what the project is.

"What are you doing with my wheels?" he asks.

"This is a big day, son. You're graduating to big boy biking! We're proud of you." And just like that, with the removal of a few screws, the training wheels fall away.

"It won't stay up now," says the boy. "It needed those wheels." He dubiously eyes the newly daunting bike.

"Sure it'll stay up," says Dad, placing an arm on his son's shoulder. "Your friend Spence rides like this. So does Ricky. Come on, I'll walk beside you while you get a feel for it. I'll be right here, see?"

The boy tentatively saddles up.

"Just a matter of balance," Dad says. "You'll get the hang of it, and it will suddenly be as easy as the old way—but a hundred times more fun." They move along, the boy pedals, and Dad tries easing his grip. Each time, the bike lurches to one side or the other and the boy gasps.

"See? It won't stay up! It'll never work!"

"Just keep *feeling* it—feeling that balance, left and right. It tips one way, you lean slightly to the other until it's steady."

"But—"

"Just try." Dad keeps it positive, keeps it encouraging. They walk along together a little more.

"Son? I'm going to remove my hands now. Get ready."

"Dad, please, *please* don't—"

Of course the inevitable happens. Dad lets go, the boy pedals once, twice, and for a splendid moment the bike seems to be cruising. Then it lurches again, and the bike spills the boy into the shrubbery along the roadside.

"Ow! I scraped my knee, Dad! I got hurt, and it's your fault!" He goes running inside, angry, crying. He's thinking that his dad will surely get it now—Mom will put him in time-out! Instead, to his shock, Mom cleans up his scrape and says, "Come on. We can't let that bike beat us, can we?"

To the boy, it's all so scary, so crazy. His folks usually are all about shielding him from the smallest scratch or scrape. They protect him from any chance of getting hurt. So why are they sending him on these crazy suicide missions on a bicycle?

Thirty minutes later, such questions are all forgotten, because the same boy is pumping the pedals like a competitor in the Tour de France. Like a Big Kid. He's shouting, laughing, feeling the tickle of the wind.

He's on top of the world. Who ever needed training wheels?

Mom and Dad stand in the driveway, sighing in relief. He takes her hand. They've survived one more rite of passage.

Has God sent you on any "suicide missions" recently? No, I'm not talking about bicycles—I'm talking about life.

Today we have a phenomenon known as the "helicopter parent." That's the mom or dad who hovers over a child at all times, past the line of protective and all the way into over-protective. What happens to a child who doesn't learn to fight his own battles? What happens if he never learns to ride the bike? To jump into the swimming pool? To eat the foods that are good for her? To drive a car or go on a date?

At some point, as we all know, the helicopters must back off and return to base. One of the toughest tasks of parenting is knowing when to let go, when to let a child take the minor bumps and bruises necessary to learn something new in life.

If you've ever raised a teenager, you have a vivid memory of that first night when your child took the car out on his own. It's terrifying! Your blood pressure would be lower if you simply made the declaration that your child would not learn to drive.

But would you be doing your job as a parent? Of course not.

Practically speaking, no parent can accompany a child every moment, all the way through life. But what if it were possible? Would it be a good idea? What would life be like for a child who never had to make a single personal decision? Never had to face a single problem? Never had to learn to do anything alone? It wouldn't be much of a life.

God knows that. One of the most important reasons that he allows hardship is the same reason Dad allows his son to fall off the bike.

Life would be sad and empty without the freedom to fail, the reality of pain, and the darkness that tells us, by comparison, what light is.

GOD IN THREE ACTS

Think about the best movie you ever saw. Try to remember the plotline. Did the hero win glory without ever facing a single bad guy? Did the lovers have a crisis-free path to happily ever after? Did the boxer easily win every single match?

If these things had been true, I think we can agree the movie would have been pretty dull. Stories are all about fighting obstacles because life has the same theme. The hero needs a mountain to climb. Lovers need obstacles in order to prove their love. Boxers need to be knocked down a few times—otherwise their glory wouldn't be too glorious at the end. It is precisely the sad or frightening moments that create a context for joy, a reason to celebrate. Without darkness, we wouldn't know what light is.

Your life is a story too—every day a new page in the narrative God is composing. He has the grace to allow you to stumble in order that you may walk and then run. Does he enjoy your pain? He does not, any more than a father enjoys seeing his son fall from a bicycle, or his daughter terrified of the swimming pool. The heavenly Father knows that struggle is one of the minimum daily requirements in the breakfast of champions. It's spiritual protein. He knows that each one of us must struggle if we're going to move to new heights and gain new wisdom; and that we must know the full meaning of defeat before we can ever savor the delicious taste of victory.

So you lost a job, or someone broke off a relationship with you, when you thought this person was *the one*. You wept, you prayed, and you fought depression, all the while asking the *Why* question. Why did God allow this to happen? Why won't he intervene now?

Let's think about some possible answers to that question. One is that he may be acting (or not acting) to *protect* you. There may be a better job or a more perfect partner out there for you, but the better future is impossible to see from your limited perspective. God may have better things in mind for you. The child can't see past the training wheels, but the parent can.

That brings us to the second possible reason for God's silence. He could be *strengthening* you. Sometimes iron simply needs to be tempered by fire; there's no other way to make it as tough as it needs to be. You've been burned, but you're going to emerge from this experience of loss as a wiser and more mature individual, because God uses these trials to teach us. You're going to know what it means to handle disappointment, and this will make victory all the sweeter later.

In the last chapter I spoke of the people from my home church who emerged from the loss of their drowned pastor as closer followers of Christ, wiser and deeper, ready for powerful ministry. The tragedy seemed to have absolutely no redeeming meaning at the moment it happened, and even for a period of years afterward. But it created a community of steel-tempered believers who accomplished great things for God.

That point, in turn, brings us to a third act of God in the midst of what seems like inaction: He could be preparing you. We see him do this over and over. You'll be in a restaurant a year from now. An old friend will walk in, someone you haven't seen in years. He'll confide that he just lost his job, and it will be as if a light switched on in your head.

> **THE HARDEST** moments of life often bear the seeds of a fruitfulness we could never foresee.

You'll feel a powerful urge to comfort and encourage, and you'll say, "You know what? A year ago I was right where you are. I thought my life was ruined, and it turned out to be—as strange as this may sound—the best thing that ever happened to me. Can we meet for coffee and talk about it?"

The hardest moments of life often bear the seeds of a fruitfulness we could never foresee.

Might I suggest that when we say, "God didn't act," we're missing something? God is *always* acting.

When we say, "God is silent," it's a good possibility we're simply tuned to the wrong frequency, because God always has something to say.

WHEN GOD SAYS YES

Let's make another point here. We've discussed the meaning of God saying no, and it would be easy to conclude that this is all he ever says. What a message for the world: "Come follow our God of silence and inaction, and here's a list of the consolation prizes."

God does say yes—he says it frequently. Part of the problem is that we don't know what to ask for. The little girl's parents say no because she asks for candy too frequently; the right to stay up too late; more toys than she could ever enjoy. As she grows, she becomes wiser and better able to ask wisely. And she hears the word *yes* more frequently.

Other times God says yes, and we may not even notice. We have a human tendency to celebrate our good fortune and think of it as no more than that—good fortune instead of *God* fortune. Bad things seem like "acts of God" to us, but when something good happens, we think, "Why not? I'm a great guy. I deserve it!"

Sometimes—more often than most of us realize—we cry out to heaven and God intervenes in exactly the way we crave. He comes through and protects us from pain after all. What is he up to on those occasions when he says yes? Did you, in fact, deserve it?

We'll never know for certain. But here's something to consider: It could just be that it's not all about you.

The purpose of God's intervention is always his own glory, which is what all the world needs. In clear and immediate intervention, the world receives a powerful reminder that he is real and he is powerful.

Jesus was a man of prayer, and he frequently glorified God through miracles. But in the garden, he prayed three times that, if it was God's will, there might be some other fate for him than the cross—that he might drink from some other "cup." God said no, even to his own Son. His purpose, we know, was again his own glory; but the cross was the necessary path that led to the open tomb.

I asked Matt Proctor, president of Ozark Christian College, where he was when the Joplin tornado hit in 2011. He told me a chilling story.

After a church youth event, Matt and his wife, Katie, were driving two dozen elementary school kids back to church. The tornado, they knew, was drawing near, so it was a race against time. Katie was at the wheel of the lead van, with her husband right behind her in another vehicle. That's when they heard the tornado sirens begin to wail for the second time. They were extremely worried, and began to pray for God's help in getting the kids to safety.

A vicious wind suddenly hit them. The wind, the rain, and the hail all began pounding the vans. Katie was straining to see through her windshield, and suddenly a great tree fell right in her path. She hit the brakes and halted just inches from the massive trunk.

Behind her, Matt stopped his own van and thought quickly. He shouted for the kids to get out, all the time calling out to God for deliverance.

The whole group made for the nearest home, pounding on the door and asking for shelter. The owner let them in and escorted them to his basement, where they stayed warm, prayed, sang songs, and told Bible stories until the storm had finally spent itself.

With the coast clear, they emerged from the house and saw the storm's path. That's when they understood they'd had a very close brush with death. If they'd continued a hundred yards beyond the fallen tree, they would have entered the path of a half-mile wide, F5 tornado that was in the process of killing 161 people.

Here is where we often try to draw simplistic generalities—they prayed and therefore God saved them; they were righteous, so they were delivered. We should be cautious. Sometimes, as we know, good people pray and God does not intervene. We can praise his name for Matt, Katie, and the two dozen children in their care, but we must also be sensitive to the truth that others died in the same disaster; some of them undoubtedly prayed too.

This is the mystery, and we must accept that the mystery endures. God won't explain his actions to us until some later time. The point here is that he does indeed intervene sometimes. If we believed that there was no point in asking God for anything, we would lose a lot of motivation to pray. But one of the most frequent commands of the New Testament is to pray, and to pray without ceasing. God does answer prayer, and he does in fact want us to share our heart's desires with him. Whether his answer is yes or no, the act of prayer itself will help to transform us.

Our main concern here, however, is those times when we struggle, when God doesn't seem to intervene. Let's turn to some strategies for walking in the light when all the world seems dark. God has a program for pain. It is never wasted, but put to invaluable use, each tear an investment in something more precious than gold.

Neither does God turn his back on us during our times of trial and suffering. We know the cliché of loving discipline: "This is going to hurt me more than it hurts you." God is compassionate. He aches with us, even as he allows the medicine to take effect. And in the meantime, He does offer an abundant array of promises to help us endure. We'll discuss three of them here.

CHASING THE SUNRISE

Jerry Sittser's book *A Grace Disguised* tells the heartbreaking story of how he lost his mother, his wife, and their youngest daughter in an automobile accident he survived. He struggled not to lose his faith as well.

Sittser, a Christian counselor, underwent terrible grief and had troubling questions for God. How could he counsel others when he needed so much help personally? The turning point came when he experienced a kind of "waking dream" of chasing the sun. It was sinking over the horizon, and he was running westward desperately after it to bring it back. But of course his efforts were in vain. The darkness swallowed him up.

Afterward, he talked to his sister, who told him the only way to catch the sun would be to turn around and run eastward into the darkness, until he met the sunrise.

Sittser writes:

> *I discovered in that moment that I had the power to choose the direction my life would head. . . . I decided from that point on to walk into the darkness rather than try to outrun it, to let my experience of loss take me on a journey wherever it would lead, and to allow myself to be transformed by my suffering rather than to think I could somehow avoid it.* [1]

One of the keys in coping with darkness is in understanding how it leads us to light.

THE PROMISE OF HIS PRESENCE

First, God promises his presence. He says, "Never will I leave you; never will I forsake you" (Hebrews 13:5).

I played Little League baseball as a youngster. Like so many boys, I was in love with everything about the game. I dreamed of playing ball someday with my heroes, Mickey Mantle and Bobby Richardson.

At nine, I had to travel four miles to practice with my team. Sometimes one of the other dads would give me a ride home after practice. Mr. Nieman would let me off at the end of the road, and I'd walk a half-mile up the gravel drive to our house. But there were days when practice went late, and I'd find myself heading home as the darkness crept in. I wasn't too happy on those later walks. The old, dusty road could be a little spooky once the sun was gone. Every rustle of a bush might be a coyote; every shadow could be an escaped convict waiting to attack me with an axe.

I'd heard all the creepy campfire stories, and I rounded that last curve for home base at a pretty good speed. But a half-mile is a long way to the plate.

During the rides, Mr. Nieman must have wondered why I was so quiet on the way home, compared to the other kids. I was watching the last rays of the sun swallowed up in the dusk. But there were a few wonderful moments. There were evenings when I spotted the silhouette of my dad, standing at the end of the road with a welcoming smile, ready to walk me home. I'll never forget what a happy sight that was for a nine-year-old. We'd walk home together, and the darkness held no more fear. Dad was by my side.

There are two ways to walk through the valley of the shadow. It can be "that lonesome road" or it can be a shared journey. God told Joshua, "Be strong and courageous. Do not be afraid; do not be discouraged, for the LORD your God will be with you wherever you go" (Joshua 1:9).

Jesus said, "I am with you always, to the very end of the age" (Matthew 28:20).

God makes no empty promises. He blows no smoke. Throughout the Scriptures we find his consistent promise to be with us. He never promises to transform the path to a rose garden, but he tells us that the darkest roads will never prevent him from walking beside us. David said, "Even though I walk through the darkest valley, I will fear no evil, for you are with me" (Psalm 23:4). David faced a giant in battle, when no one else had the courage. He spent years hiding in the wilderness from the army of a king who was hunting him like prey. He endured God's discipline and later, the pain of his own errors as a father. Through all these things, he was a man after God's own heart because he always took courage in God's presence. His Dad was with him, and he could face the darkness.

I like the familiar plaque that reads, "Lord, help me to remember that there is nothing that's going to happen to me today that you and I can't handle together." Regardless of what happens, the Lord will be there to walk that hardest half-mile, down the dark road, his loving arm around your shoulder.

THE PROMISE OF HIS MATURITY

Secondly, as we've already mentioned, God is at work within us through our suffering. He is strengthening us, giving us depth, wisdom, perspective. The Bible tells us that testing is the process of making us "mature and complete, not lacking anything" (James 1:4).

Paul writes, "We also glory in our sufferings, because we know that suffering produces perseverance; perseverance, character; and character, hope" (Romans 5:3–4). In other words, there is a gradual, almost imperceptible process—a chain reaction of maturing—that is triggered by the pain we endure. Suffering teaches us to hang on. Hanging on teaches us character. And character establishes powerful hope. Who would ever think that the end result of pain was hope?

But that's Jesus—Jesus who specializes in turning our expectations upside down. There was a time when he asked his friends to climb into a boat and make for the other side of the Sea of Galilee, where he would join them later. That night, the skies grew dark as they rowed the little boat. A great storm churned up. Some of these men were fishermen and knew what it was like to be in the wrong waters at the wrong time. They fought the storm with all their considerable strength, but man against nature is always a losing battle. At the end of their endurance, they began to face the prospect of going under the dark waters and not coming up.

It was then that hope emerged in the least likely way. Christ came walking to them across the waves. Equally startling, he calmed the storm with a mere command. We have no power against the forces of nature or adversity of any kind—but he is the ruler over all things. And he is still in the business of calming storms.

A friend of our family went through a nasty divorce a few years ago. She discovered that her husband had been cheating on her repeatedly, and that he had no intention of changing his ways. Our friend was a wonderful Christian woman who did everything in her power to save her marriage. Like the disciples, she fought the storm valiantly. Finally, in her exhaustion, she had no path but that of separation from a husband who could not be faithful.

After a few years, she met a godly man, and the two married and now serve together as missionaries in Eastern Europe. When I ask her about the years of pain and divorce, she smiles and tells me this: "Never in my life did I grow so deeply as I did during that time of pain. God did an incredible work within me in a relatively short time—but I never want to grow that quickly again!"

Many of us understand exactly what she means: It was the best of times, it was the worst of times; it was a gift of God she couldn't do without, and one she hopes she won't need to "do with" anytime soon.

A mother goes through the pain of childbirth, but she holds on to the hope of the beautiful newborn child, sent from heaven, that the pain makes possible. When we're hurting, it helps to know that we're investing toward becoming the remarkable, fruitful servants of God that he wants us to be.

THE PROMISE OF HEAVEN

Finally, God promises that this era of suffering is only temporary. We are actually citizens of heaven. Our home is the presence of God, in a new world in which all things will be made right by him.

The Bible, God's eternal Word, ends with a glimpse of that reality, which is too marvelous for our finite minds to grasp. In Revelation 21, John sees a vision of the new heaven and new earth. A loud voice from heaven cries,

> *"Look! God's dwelling place is now among the people, and he will dwell with them. They will be his people, and God himself will be with them and be their God. 'He will wipe every tear from their eyes. There will be no more death' or mourning or crying or pain, for the old order of things has passed away."*
> —Revelation 21:3–4

Christ then declares that he is making everything new, that his great work is accomplished, and that those who love him will receive their reward.

It isn't a dream; it's a reality, a solid promise from God. Think of the health challenges you have today. No matter what they are, you will outlive them. Your biggest, most unsolvable problems are living on borrowed time, while you are not. Your day of redemption draws near.

On that great day—so much closer than any of us realize, since this life passes quickly—we will be given new and perfect bodies. There will be no more high blood pressure, no more cancer, no more colds, no more debilitating diseases. People who have spent their entire lives in wheelchairs will walk and run and jump for joy. Those blind for life will open their eyes and see perfect light, a full spectrum nobody on this earth has beheld. The deaf will break in their new ears with the glorious music of the forever kingdom.

And there will be a permanent reunion of the human family—spouses, parents, children, and friends once separated by death, embracing again, together once and for all.

Abraham lived a nomadic life in tents for decades, and what kept him going was this promise of a better life. "He was looking forward to the city with foundations, whose architect and builder is God" (Hebrews 11:10).

Moses lived a dusty, crisis-laden wilderness life among an unruly nation, and what kept him going was the reality of an eternal promised land: "He chose to be mistreated along with the people of God rather than to enjoy the fleeting pleasures of sin . . . because he was looking ahead to his reward" (Hebrews 11:25–26).

And then there was Joseph.

Joseph is one of the most fascinating characters in ancient history. The Bible goes into great detail about his life, a case study of suffering, faith, and how God interacts with us in our struggles. Throughout this book, we'll find that the experiences of Joseph offer a running commentary on the issues we discuss. Several thousand years separate his time and ours, and yet so little has changed! We fight the same battles as Joseph, and therefore we have the opportunity to take hold of his lessons and be victorious.

Joseph faced particularly vicious betrayal by family members—and he survived.

He faced sexual temptation without giving in—and he only earned false accusation.

In prison, he helped out a friend—only to be forgotten by the friend when it counted.

God tested him to the limit and beyond, because God knew that within Joseph were the seeds of powerful faith. Joseph could have given up; he could have turned bitter and vengeful. Instead, he took the hand of God, walked his dark road, and found a day of glory.

Corrie ten Boom once said that there is no pit so deep that the love of God is not deeper still. Is it true? Can we really live with such a profound guarantee of winning out in the end?

Joseph would tell us the answer is a joyful *yes*. And you'll see it not only because one figure from history found the way, but because that figure offers a blueprint for how you and I can do the same.

TWO WORDS

We've looked at the promises of God that can bear us up in our days of darkness. As we close this chapter, I also want to offer two words that are keys to insight.

The first is *time*.

Perhaps today is one of those *Why* moments for you. You're experiencing pain and frustration, all the while wondering why God does not intervene. What possible good could come from what you're going through?

THE BIBLE tells us that through time, God makes all things beautiful.

Take hold of the concept of time. The Bible tells us that through time, God makes all things beautiful. He casts light that chases away every shred of darkness. We know that with God, a thousand years is as a day and a day is like a thousand years (2 Peter 3:8). This is because he does not live within time and the tyranny of ticking clocks, as we do. We reside completely in the present moment, past behind us, future before us. God is not thus limited, because time is simply something he created. He sees the entire canvas of a vast painting, while we can only see the tiniest brushstroke.

His promise is that one day you, too, will stand back from that painting and see the breathtaking picture he was painting. You will realize there were wonderful reasons and purposes for all things, but that your task was simply to wait on God. To be faithful—and to trust.

That's the second word I'd like to offer you: *trust*. Jesus said, "Do not let your hearts be troubled. You believe in God; believe also in me. My Father's house has many rooms; if that were not so, would I have told you that I am going there to prepare a place for you?" (John 14:1–2).

He made that statement to a roomful of anxious friends, who felt the tension in the air of marching Roman soldiers, angry religious authorities, bloodthirsty mobs who were surely coming to seize Jesus at any moment. His statement to his friends, including us, is, "Trust me! Haven't you seen how I care for you? Don't you know that I can calm any storm and turn it to my own purposes? If you could only see the room I've laid out for you. *Trust me.*"

GREAT rewards lie in wait for those who persevere.

Great rewards lie in wait for those who persevere. If we could only see that now, we wouldn't need so much faith to get through the hard times. But of course, faith-building is the whole point. Job, the great suffering soul of the Old Testament, said that even if God took his life, still he would trust him. That's ultimate faith, isn't it, the kind you and I strive for? And it's easier for us, because, you see, we can see the end result. We see the cross. God offered the life of his own Son, and the result was resurrection. The result was that death was defeated.

God is trustworthy. His love is far more than our small minds can comprehend. Therefore we take hold of time and trust, and we place our hope in him. That's called night vision.

QUESTIONS FOR YOU

1. What personal experience did the opening bicycle story remind you of? What lessons did you learn at the time?

2. The first of three "acts of God" is his protection of us. How can protection seem like persecution? How has this been illustrated in your experience?

3. What is the difference between the other two acts, strengthening and preparation? How does each function?

4. What promises does God offer us for times of suffering? Which seems to you the most powerful, and why?

5. What insights did you gain about time and trust as aids for night vision? Which one means the most to you?

6. Can you think of any time in your life when you needed to experience darkness to help you recognize light?

3: SUFFER THE CHILDREN

Where Is God in a Hurting Home?

I'VE BEEN A PASTOR for many years. That means that sometimes I still hear the echoes—echoes of voices I've heard in counseling through the years. The pain still comes across, as I lie in bed late at night and remember the anxious faces in my office.

So many kinds of pain. So many family disruptions:

> I've got this sister who just won't help out. You see, our mother has Alzheimer's. We did put her in an extended care unit, but soon she may have to move to the lockdown unit. There are things that have to be done, decisions to be made, and my sister just says she doesn't want to remember Mom that way.
>
> We married in our late twenties, and we'd waited in order to be pure on our wedding night. Then, by our late thirties, we knew we couldn't have children. It's ironic, isn't it? We were obedient to God; meanwhile, we watch couples having children out of wedlock, young women having abortions without even thinking about it—what's up with that?
>
> I worshiped my dad; I would have always said we were pretty close. When it all came out—that he'd been having an affair with some woman at work for twenty years—it knocked the breath out of me. All those business trips? Lies. He was cheating on Mom, cheating on us, all that time. Now this

woman has inherited some money and they've run off together, leaving my mom alone on a fixed income. She always trusted God, and she deserves better.

My wife and I applied for adoption. That means money, patience, anxiety. We prayed, we waited upon God, and we gave thanks the day we received a baby girl from Ukraine—only to discover there were problems with her brain. Now she's ten, we love her, but her life will be so limited. Sometimes we can't help but dream of the bright, talented children we might have had. Am I evil for thinking those thoughts?

Two questions for you.

First, how did you picture the speakers of those four narratives? I'll correct myself: *speaker*. For yes, all these thoughts came from one man.

He sat in my office and described his family concerns, past, present, and future. Family was everything to him, and yet it had been such a rugged road, from the family he was born into, to the one he began. Even very good families suffer; innocent children bear the burden of their parents' confusion.

Second question: What would you predict about the current faith of the man who said these things?

Would you be surprised to hear that he is as dedicated to God, and as joyful, as ever? He'll be quick to tell you he has a list of questions for God, and he'll be quick to voice them when he arrives in heaven. He's been angry with God more than a few times. But he's wise. He never assumes that a loving God means an easy life. Jesus never said he was the Comfortable Shepherd—just the good one.

> **FAMILY** pain is excruciating pain by definition, because it hits us where we live.

As a matter of fact, my friend sees the harshness of life as his training ground in that very goodness. "Only God can sustain me," he says.

"If I hadn't crawled through the low points of life, I'd never come to the high points of trusting in God. I know how good he is, and I trust his plan."

His example inspires me. It teaches me how to experience God more deeply through my own trials. But that's hard, isn't it? Particularly in the area of family. The home is ground zero in our lives. It's our sanctuary and fortress. Family pain is excruciating pain by definition, because it hits us where we live. And no matter how far we've followed Jesus through life, there comes the time when we wonder *why*.

Which brings us back around to the story of Joseph.

ENCOUNTERING JOSEPH

There's a reason that so many of us name Joseph as our favorite Old Testament character. His story is a barn-burner, a page-turner, and it plays out across fifteen chapters of Genesis with never a dull moment. It has action, intrigue, heartbreak, redemption, and everything we'd want in a classic story.

It's also the hinge on which the fate of Israel turns. The entire nation and its future were transformed by the acts of this one man. But even if he'd been an obscure character rather than a prince and patriarch, we'd still be fascinated by this character—Joseph and the messy, tangled family that launched him into the world.

From the first few sentences of Genesis 37, as he enters the biblical narrative, we see the young man's imperfections. Frankly, we find him a little obnoxious. Yet as we turn the pages, he will grow, before our very eyes, to the embodiment of powerful faith; of a case study in stubborn faith. If a spoiled brat can become a man of wisdom and courage, what does that imply for you and me?

Joseph becomes a unique Old Testament hero. Keep in mind: Noah got drunk. Abraham lied. Jacob scammed and schemed. Moses murdered, and David committed adultery before having the woman's husband killed. And these were the greatest names in those pages.

Joseph, who probably suffered more than all of them combined, never faltered when the heat was on him. He continued to trust and obey. Maybe it was for that very reason: his suffering crystallized his faith. There was every reason for his soul to grow as dark as the dungeon where they disposed of him; every reason for him to give in to bitterness. But Joseph trusted God until the moment when all that trust paid off.

Before all of that, of course, he began life as a child of privilege—just one more spoiled kid in a dysfunctional family.

Of course we live in the age of the dysfunctional family. When I was young, you didn't hear that term; now we all know what it means, and we see them all around us. Counselors have their definitions: families with excessive hurt, producing a lack of respect and a sense of disintegration.

But let's break it down more simply. We're talking about a home that has lost its godly purpose. The Lord designed the family to be an oasis of security, love, and harmony, a place of strength and joy; a factory manufacturing young lives of brilliance. A dysfunctional home becomes something close to the opposite. It breaks down rather than fortifying. It produces despair rather than hope, bitterness rather than joy.

A family counselor reading Genesis 37 would catch several red-flag phrases, and conclude that this was a family bound to struggle.

RED FLAGS IN THE SUNSET

The first red flag is simple enough: "Joseph, a young man of seventeen" (v. 2). Adolescence is the great family battlefield, the time when parents and children may truly lock horns for the first time. Teenagers are fascinated and compelled by independence. Doors lock, communication chills, and Mom and Dad begin to wonder what happened to the sweet child they knew on the other side of puberty.

It's completely normal and completely unnerving. As a young person tries on a new and different body, and explores the world with more knowing eyes, conflict is inevitable—even for the most naturally sunny and obedient kids.

Fourteen was the magic age for me: I had been everything my parents wanted, and then, suddenly, they couldn't figure out what had gotten into me. They had been praying for me to become a preacher; now they could only pray that I'd hang on to my faith, period, and stay out of trouble.

Consider this. We have only one quick glimpse of Jesus during his adolescent years, and even the perfect Son of God is seen ruffling his parents' feathers. At twelve, he is lost on a trip to Jerusalem. He asserts his independence, taking off to consult the teachers of the Law at the temple. Then, when his anxious parents find him, he says, "Why were you looking for me? Didn't you know I had to be in my father's house?" I hear a little teen-speak in there, don't you?

The Bible tells us his parents "did not understand what he meant by that" (Luke 2:50). If Joseph and Mary were puzzled by such a son, then you and I are in pretty good company. We know all about the feeling that our loving children have wandered off, that they don't seem to need us anymore.

The second red flag is in the phrase, "his father's wives" (v. 2). Note the plural. Jacob, the father of Joseph, has been deceived into marrying two sisters, one of whom he adores and one of whom he never asked for. Their father has pulled a fast one, getting seven extra years of labor out of Jacob, who is given Leah instead of Rachel after working seven years to earn her. Dad knows that if the young man was good for seven, he will be good for fourteen—and finally Jacob, sadder but wiser, has two wives on his hands after all those years.

It's another example of how *not* to parent: A father has set up his own daughters for misery. For predictably, there is bitter competition between the two women. Leah is heartbroken, craving a love she is never given. Her ill feelings will become a legacy that carries down to the next generation.

Jacob fathers six sons by Leah, two by Rachel, and even four by two of his servants—a blended family. It takes incredible wisdom and grace to pull together such a group, but sadly, Jacob doesn't show that grace. He is clear in his favoritism toward Joseph and Benjamin, the sons of Rachel. The rest of them he treats as "also-rans," just as their mothers are afterthoughts to him. And they watch with deep resentment. Nothing good will come of such a situation.

That brings us to yet another red flag, found in verse 3, where we're told that Jacob "loved Joseph more than any of his other sons."

Joseph, of course, is Rachel's first son, and he comes along during Jacob's "sunset" years. He has wanted a son by his favorite wife for many years, and finally come Joseph and then Benjamin.

Have you ever noticed that parents can be far more relaxed and lenient with the kids who are born last? We hover over our first children, but the rules become just a little softer with each new arrival. The Bible tells us that Jacob lets his older sons do all the heavy lifting, while Joseph is doted upon and favored. You might remember the story of the ornamented robe. We have called it the "coat of many colors" in children's Bible stories, but the best translation of the phrase suggests it is a richly decorated garment.

Joseph flaunts his threads, intentionally irritating his brothers. He's the golden boy, he knows it, and he is determined to make that an issue.

Imagine one of today's fathers who gives each of his kids a cellphone at the age of twelve. But when his favorite son reaches that age, he gives him the latest iPad with all the frills—along with the cellphone. How do you think the siblings are going to take it?

The Bible tells us: "They hated him" (v. 4).

Two further red flags are here in Genesis 37:

First, moving. Jacob has recently uprooted his family and moved back to Canaan, the land where he was a child. This suggests he is at a time of life when he's looking back, rather than focusing on his family and its future. Moving is often necessary, but it can be tough on families.

Second, Rachel has died while giving birth to Joseph's little brother Benjamin. As a matter of fact, Joseph has also lost his grandfather Isaac. He and his father are both grieving.

Thus Jacob's clan is experiencing a kind of perfect storm of family conflict. The Bible is a far more contemporary book than some people think, isn't it?

NOT SO SWEET DREAMS

Life for a blended family can be challenging. Perhaps you've been there. If not, you can easily think of friends or relatives in such a situation. Sometimes, when the parents are loving and gentle, there can be smooth sailing. Other times, the waters are far more turbulent and precarious. There is competition and resentment.

A Bible college president recently confided that half the students studying for ministry in his school come from what we often call broken homes. It's simply the state of our culture. We can expect these young, budding ministers to have a special compassion for those who have struggled in their upbringing. On the other hand, they may have to minister without good models of family wisdom from their own background. We know that people are prone to struggle with the same issues that troubled their parents.

As we look at Joseph, we have the advantage of knowing the kind of man he was destined to become. Can we look at our own children, or some of the troubled youth around us, and manage to see who they *can* be rather than simply who they are right now? In other words, can we see people the way God sees them?

Joseph was on his way to greatness, but he had a few miles yet to travel. He was vain and egotistical. He seems to have had something of a chip on his shoulder. In verse 5 of Genesis 37, for example, he can't wait to tell them his latest dream, in which all the brothers are binding sheaves of grain. His sheaf stands regally while the others—one for each of his siblings—bows down to it.

No psychiatrist was necessary to interpret that particular dream. The brothers are outraged at Joseph's arrogance, and their hatred spirals.

Again, we can see the future—we know how this story comes out, and how the dream is a true one. It comes from God. That doesn't mean Joseph is supposed to make an issue out of it. Just because God blesses us in some way, it doesn't mean it's time for us to show off. Blessings, as a matter of fact, should humble us. They should put us in our place, showing us that whatever we have, we wouldn't have it without a loving God who lavishes wonderful gifts upon us.

Joseph could be and should be awed by the dream he has had. If he's going to be in a position of authority, he'll have to be ready for it. Big things will be required of him. Of course, he doesn't have the maturity to see it that way. Instead, it's just more bright apparel to flaunt before his brothers. He confuses his future standing in the dream with his present standing. And that's a mistake he'll pay for.

I remember my freshman year in college. When I checked into the dorm, I brought along some athletic trophies I'd won in high school. I was proud of them, of course, and I placed them on a high shelf where anyone who walked in would spot them.

I smiled whenever I glanced in that direction, until the day I noticed a new one sitting with the other hardware—a little trophy with a plaque reading, "World's Greatest Ballplayer."

An upperclassman was sending a not-so-subtle message that bragging is particularly unwelcome in college freshmen. As I realized I was making myself look conceited, I was embarrassed and in a hurry to wipe away that impression. The trophies discreetly found their way into a box. It hurts to be knocked down a peg, but it's a good hurt. It brings emotional growth.

As Joseph's brothers sizzle, he only makes things worse. He has a similar dream (nothing less than the sun, moon, and stars bowing before him this time) and he broadcasts the highlights again. Maybe—just maybe—Joseph is a paranoid turned inside out. That is, he's certain everyone's out to do him good, and doesn't realize he's antagonizing his siblings.

I doubt it. It's much easier to see in Joseph the typical spoiled teenager who doesn't have enough chores to keep him busy, and alleviates his boredom by picking at those around him.

TIME OUT FOR A FISH STORY

As a matter of fact, I can see just a hint of my own sons in Joseph's story.

One day I took my two sons fishing. I baited the hook for Phil, who was six, and he threw his line into the water. You know how beginner's luck works in fishing; almost immediately, the first grader got one on his line. "I got one! I got one!" he shouted in exhilaration.

His brother Rusty was ten at the time. "Way to go, Phil," he said with a smile. "Way to go."

It was a nice fish. I re-baited Phil's hook, he threw in the line, and the tug came within seconds. "I got another one! I got another one!"

Big brother Rusty was paying close attention now. He came over, threw his line in the same spot, and quickly there was a catch—not for Rusty but for his little brother. It was Phil's third conquest. Boy, he had this fishing thing licked. He looked at Rusty and said, "I got three!" He held up three fingers and then said it again.

It was working on Rusty pretty effectively. There's just nothing in life like being outdone by your little brother. Rusty looked at me and quietly said, "Dad, can you bait my hook, too?"

It was a good idea, but it didn't help. "I got five!" That's what we were hearing a few minutes later. "I got five, Russ, how many you got?"

You could almost see the steam coming out of Rusty's ears. "Dad," he said, "tell Phil to shut up."

"Don't say, 'shut up,' son," I said. Then I turned to the little guy. "Be quiet, Phil," I said. "You've said more than enough. You're making your brother angry."

But Phil was riding too high to be shot down. He just couldn't leave it alone. He made up a song that went,

> *I went fishing and I caught five fish.*
> *I went fishing and I caught five fish.*
> *I went fishing and I caught five fish . . .*

"Dad—make him stop singing that song."

"Phil," I said, "don't sing that song anymore." So he stopped singing it. Instead, he *hummed* it in such a way that his brother was sure to hear it. By now, Rusty had just about reached his limit. His little brother was baiting him more than any fish.

I said, "Phil, don't even hum it." A minute later, I looked over and saw him bopping his head to the beat, mouthing the lyrics, and Rusty, needless to say, was staring daggers at him. There's something in the nature of sibling rivalry, isn't there? Just an irresistible impulse to push any advantage to its limit. And the jealousy it provokes is as old as Cain and Abel.

I wonder if Joseph had his own little song:

> *I went to sleep and had a dream.*
> *I went to sleep and had a dream.*
> *I went to sleep and had a dream,*
> *Showed I'm the coach and you're the team.*

If he didn't, we can be sure that, like Phil, he found every possible way to rub salt in the wound.

The problem in Joseph's situation is that Jacob isn't there to say, "Don't say it, don't sing it, don't hum it, and don't even bop your head." The patriarch of the family is busy with other things. Meanwhile, Joseph is pushing the limit, pushing the limit some more, and all the evidence tells the brothers that those dreams are more than talk.

Old Jacob will make Joseph the boss someday, because Joseph is his pet. And the wheels are turning in the heads of the brothers—something must be done.

FACING THE COLD, HARD TRUTH

Genesis includes this summary about Joseph's situation: "His brothers were jealous of him, but his father kept the matter in mind" (v. 11).

Dad needs to do more than "keep it in mind." He needs to be proactive.

But soon comes the fateful day when he sends Joseph with a care package for the other sons, who are off a ways tending sheep. Maybe he believes the care package will put Joseph in a better light, but the situation is much more dangerous than the boys' father realizes. Because when you're far from home, anything can happen.

We as parents can't afford to be naïve about our kids and the world they live in. Maybe we just don't want to face the unsettling truth. We need to realize that this world is not a kid-friendly place. More than that, we need to face the hard truth about our kids. They're at a confusing juncture of life. They're torn in many directions, and they're not as good as we want to think they are.

How many of us have said, "My child would never do that!" Are we really sure?

Teenagers are capable of deceiving us. Their hormones are on overdrive, their friends are competing to see who can push the boundaries the hardest, and the world today is a laboratory for new kinds of evil. Jacob sends his seventeen-year-old son out into a wilderness, and we often do just the same. We can't afford to place them in harm's way.

Phil, one-time fishing phenomenon, is now a sergeant in the police department, catching some big ones, as it turns out. But his stories aren't lighthearted. He tells me about lax parents who leave their kids at home for days on end as they take their vacations and do whatever their thing may be. Many moms and dads today fail to see parenting as their central charge in life.

These parents have no clue that their teens are at home having parties filled with drugs, drink, and sex. When the police inevitably get involved, the parents' first impulse is to defend their kids. They tell the police they're overreacting. "Kids will be kids," they say. "Weren't you ever young?"

They arrive home to see the undeniable evidence, and then they can only blame their kids' friends—*they're* the bad apples, it's all *their* fault. These adults see and think what they want to see and think.

I don't remember my mom that way at all; she let us know exactly where the limits were, and also the consequences of going beyond them. "When we're gone, don't you ever bring your girlfriend into this house," Mom would say, and the look in her eye said, *I mean business.*

I tested the boundaries, as kids do: "Don't you trust me, Mom?"

"No," she would say. She didn't have a naïve bone in her body.

I would pretend to be deeply wounded. "My own mom doesn't trust me," I would moan. But as I walked away, my thoughts were, *That woman is pretty savvy.*

Serious parents take the Bible seriously. The Bible happens to teach that we're all members of the human race, created in God's image but fallen and damaged. We are born with a sin nature. If someone ever tells you that children are a "blank slate," innocent and perfect until their parents gently write upon that slate, know that this person is flying in the face not only of biblical revelation, but of simple human observation.

Children inherit a sin legacy. No one is more self-centered than a child. It requires wise, gracious, and firm discipline on the part of parents to bring that sin nature under at least some control—but only Jesus Christ can save and cleanse our children as they become older.

Until they themselves become wise, obedient followers of Christ as young adults—assuming things go as they should—we must be, as Jesus says, "shrewd as snakes and as innocent as doves" (Matthew 10:16). Love guides us, but that love understands the place of facing facts and imposing discipline.

Facing facts means checking your kids' rooms. It means being vigilant over their usage of technology—computers, smartphones, video games. It means keeping an eye on their choices for friends and activities. You're the family shepherd, and to repeat what we've said before, being a good shepherd doesn't mean being an easy one. The shepherd does what he must to protect his flock. It's no different for you as a parent.

THE DIGITAL JUNGLE

A 2012 study of teenagers and the Internet showed an alarming trend: Parents aren't engaged with the online activity of their children—yet they believe the opposite to be true.

Parents are saying, "We've got this."

Kids are saying, "Our parents have no clue."

For example:

- 71 percent of teenagers (up from 45 percent two years earlier) have taken action to hide their online activity from their parents.
- 48 percent of parents believe their teens tell them everything they do in cyberspace.
- 33 percent of teens admit to viewing pornography on the Internet; only 10 percent of parents are aware of it.

- 22 percent of teens have cheated on a test using their mobile phones.
- Teens spend five hours per day online; parents guess the figure is three hours.

The study's conclusion: "Parents must be jolted out of their complacency. A huge gap exists between what teens are doing online and what parents really know."[2]

CRISIS POINT

Jacob, of course, is making any number of mistakes as a parent. And he manages the greatest muff of all when he sends Joseph out—"a sheep among wolves," again in the language of Matthew 10:16. The tragic irony is that Jacob has been fully devoted to sheltering and pampering his and Rachel's boy. He wants an easy life for his two youngest sons. It looks a lot like love, but disconnected parenting isn't lovely in its consequences. Soon, the symbol of this irony will be an ornamented coat smeared in blood.

Joseph is on a trip to see his resentful brothers. It's a fifty-mile jaunt, and in a pasture near Dothan they finally see him coming. "Here comes that dreamer," they say (v. 19). The Hebrew meaning of the word is "dream expert." Pure sarcasm. Their moment has come to put little brother in his place. They talk of murdering him, throwing him in a cistern, and giving out a story that some wild animal did the deed. Let the dream expert become a nightmare expert.

Anyone who has been around dogs knows that they become very different in packs. There is a mob psychology that extends to animals. Or perhaps it's better to say that it extends from animals to people. When we become part of a mob, we'll do things we would never do by ourselves. It happens among college students at parties, drunks in a bar, soldiers on a battlefield, and even fans at a ball game. Groups intensify the likelihood of evil. It's something else to think about as we, the parents, keep an eye on the groups our kids gravitate toward.

Reuben, the oldest brother, takes positive leadership, and his action here is crucial. He at least manages to negotiate the group down to abandonment rather than outright murder. "We'll just leave him in the cistern," he says, "and we won't have his blood on our hands that way." Reuben's true intention, the Bible hints, is to slip back later and set his brother free. He knows the brothers are out of control, and he figures that the whole thing will blow over if he contrives to let Joseph live to see another day. And maybe Joseph will learn something, too.

For now, Joseph is roughed up, shoved from one brother to another, and called some names. The robe is ripped off, he is thrown into the hole, and the brothers sit and casually enjoy their meal as their brother cries for help. These are hardened men. They dip the coat in the blood of a goat and prepare their story of a boy torn apart by wolves or lions. In other words, they're going to break their father's heart. In many ways, of course, he has broken theirs. It's the cycle of generational sin.

We come, then, to a crisis point in the story of Joseph. The birds have come home to roost. This is the picture of a family at the threshold of chaos. The father—already grieving his precious wife and father—is about to lose his favorite son. We can presume that all his mistakes will leap into the forefront of his mind as he looks at the blood-smeared robe he has given his son.

He shouldn't have sent the boy so far from home, he'll reflect. He shouldn't have been so inattentive. If only . . . if only.

And could it also be that Jacob, once known for his own shrewdness, will detect some furtive spark in the eyes of his sons? Will he spend years wondering if the wild animal story is true? Remember, he has seen the hatred, and he has kept it in mind. Maybe the worst of all of it would be the wondering: Is my son really dead, and if so—could it have been fratricide?

For a parent, nothing can be crueler than golden years when the gold is tarnished by regret. God has appointed you as a guide during the most treacherous climb of a young life. As a matter of fact, pastor and author Rob Rienow compares parenting teens to scaling Mount Everest.

It costs $60,000, he says, to hire Sherpa guides on the climb. You start out the long upward trek, and the first days are the easiest and sunniest. You're doing great. Within a few days, you come to that place that is 26,000 feet above sea level. It's the beginning of what they call the "death zone." If something bad happens, this is the range.

Imagine that your Sherpa guides now tell you that they're so impressed with your skills, they're heading back to base camp and you're on your own. Wouldn't you be angry about this? The next few days are essentially what you paid all that money for. This is the hard part, and you're going to need guidance.[3]

Adolescence is the "hard part" of parenting, the place where things go wrong. It would make no sense for parents to turn back now, simply to assume that their childhood performance guarantees they'll be flawless teens. And as much as we perceive our sons and daughters asking for privacy and pushing us away, know that they want our help more than ever. One of their greatest deceptions of all is to convince you—and themselves—that they can go it alone now. More than ever, deep inside them, they know they need Mom and Dad. Keep climbing with them. Push for the top, because the glory of that is worth all the heartache that contributes to it.

In the next chapter, we'll be examining just how you can do that.

QUESTIONS FOR YOU

1. How did your own parents provide models—good or less so—of attentive guidance? Offer examples.

2. As we read Joseph's story, we're aware he is destined for greatness. Why do you think God allows him to get off to such a rocky start?

3. Which of the "red flag" warnings in the narrative of Joseph do you find most significant? Why? Which ones are most prevalent today?

4. What are some reasons that many parents fail to face reality when it comes to the dangers their children confront?

5. What practical steps can you take to be more closely engaged with the lives of your children?

4: BLESS THIS MESS

Help for Troubled Homes

IN FOOTBALL, A GOOD defensive end is a master of disaster. He has the perfect combination of size and speed. Most of all, he has a knack for creating chaos in the opponent's backfield and destroying a play before it gets going.

We had a couple of good ones on my high school team. Daniel and Pat were gifted athletes and popular students at school. Sadly, they were also products of very imperfect families. As courageous as they were in their plights, as positive as they attempted to be, I could always sense the pain that lived inside them.

Daniel's home had long since become a broken one. He lived with his mom and saw his alcoholic father only occasionally—but at just the wrong times. For example, one evening his dad came to our football game highly intoxicated, pacing the sidelines while calling out misguided "encouragements" to his son.

During the game, I glanced at Daniel and saw tears glistening inside his helmet—the broken spirit inside the gilded armor. He loved his dad even as he was humiliated by him.

As for Pat, his parents had stayed together, even as war raged between them. Shouting, physical abuse—the battle never ended. Pat's dad was arrested at his son's football practice after shoving his wife down the steps on the previous evening, breaking her arm.

Pat didn't know quite how to respond. He tried poking fun at the police, playing off the whole thing as high comedy. But we weren't fooled. For a teenage boy's life, this was the worst experience imaginable. We rallied around our two friends, offering friendship and support. But even good friends can't make up for a home gone toxic. The two fathers were creating chaos in their families as the boys created chaos in opposing backfields. But what happened at home was no game.

The most frightening realization comes when we read those ominous words from the Old Testament about

IF WE blow it with our kids, is that a forever thing?

three and four generations of children being punished for "the sin of the fathers" (Deuteronomy 5:9). In other words, we run up the debt, our kids pay the bill. And that only brings us back to the theme of this book: *Why?* Why would God oversee such a system? Why must the innocent bear the burden of parental error?

Yet we know it's true; we see it with our very eyes. Alcoholic parents are far more likely to raise alcoholic children. Kids who witness abuse may one day be prone to commit their own. Sin is the legacy none of us wish to leave, but it is quite real and quite viral.

I've shared my memory of Daniel and Pat because I want to make a point about the end results. If we blow it with our kids, is that a forever thing? Let's look at the two defensive ends, five decades later.

First, Daniel. He rose from the ashes of his heartbreak to become an outstanding educator, a faithful husband of over forty-five years, and the father of two great kids.

Meanwhile, Pat's life fell into a cycle of arrests for dealing drugs, multiple marriages, alienation from his offspring, and a lifelong battle with chemical addiction.

Where is the fork in the road between the paths of Daniel and Pat? It's actually a series of forks, which is to say the sum total of life choices. Joseph sat in a deep hole—literally—with a choice to make about his view of God going forward. His brothers had just made a terrible choice, and they would face other decisions. Jacob, too, had to decide what kind of father to be on the other side of tragic news.

How are we going to react to our pain? Will we redouble our courage and build a life of hope, or will we become embittered victims? We know what Joseph decided, because his actions bore testimony to his spirit.

Only you and I will choose the paths we walk.

HOW TO EXASPERATE YOUR CHILDREN

Every parent has quoted the commandment to their children: "Honor your father and mother." Paul quotes it in the New Testament, then adds a line that parents sometimes miss: "Fathers, do not exasperate your children; instead, bring them up in the training and instruction of the Lord" (Ephesians 6:4). *Exasperate* means to provoke to anger.

I was thinking of ways that parents exasperate, and I easily came up with nine. I know you can add to the list. If you're a parent, and you want to build your children's anger and drive them away, here are the actions on your part that will get it done:

1. Belittle them.
2. Punish based on your anger, rather than disciplining based on their needs.
3. Set unrealistic goals for them.
4. Be too lenient with them.
5. Break your promises.
6. Be grudging with the time you give them.
7. Fail to love their mother.
8. Be a hypocrite. Let them hear you say one thing and do another.

9. Fail to be the spiritual leader in your home.

OK, all of us parents see ourselves in that list. If you want to undo some of the damage those actions inflict, try this one. Think of the thing you would most like to have heard your parents say to you, then say something similarly affirming to your child. Then do the opposite of each of those nine.

BROTHERS AND CISTERN

We left Joseph in quite a predicament—as did his brothers.

Joseph is in a cistern, a kind of ditch or reservoir for collecting water. His brothers are enjoying a meal and discussing his fate. For Joseph, this is a horrendous moment that has surely changed his view of what can happen in the world. He has been pampered and spoiled, and suddenly he is sitting in a shallow grave listening to a group of men discussing whether to murder him.

Suddenly the brothers hear strangers approaching in the distance. They look up to see a caravan of Ishmaelites coming from Gilead. These are known to be slave traders, heading in the direction of Egypt.

Judah is the first to voice a new idea: Who says crime doesn't pay? If they sell their brother, they can make a tidy sum. And so it happens that Joseph is sold for twenty shekels of silver, a mid-range price for a slave of that time.

For Joseph, it could have been worse—as in *death* worse. If those slave traders don't come along in the nick of time, his life ends right there. But the nick of time is God's favorite hour of the day. G. K. Chesterton once said that what we call coincidences are "spiritual puns." A pun is a word with a double meaning, and a coincidence is an event with two meanings. Who supplies the second one? God is always working toward his divine purposes—purposes no one but he can see in the limited view of the moment. He has a purpose for Joseph, and the history of a nation hinges upon it. He has a purpose for everyone in this story—everyone in your story.

The Bible, like life itself, is packed with "it just so happened" moments. It just so happened that Ruth was gleaning in a field owned by Boaz. It just so happened that Samson was bound to the two load-supporting pillars of the temple he pulled down. It just so happened that Caesar Augustus issued a decree for taxation, requiring a man named Joseph to go to the town Jesus was decreed by prophecy to be born into. And it just so happened that Esther married a king and had the opportunity to save the Jewish people. "Just so happened" moments are what the Bible calls "in the fullness of time." Like the seasons, like the tides, there is a rhythm and a timing for everything God has planned to do.

What about for you? How often has some "coincidence" led to a fork in the road of your life? A new career? A meeting with your future spouse? When I was a young man, it just so happened that I attended a conference and noticed a pretty coed singing in a girls' trio. It just so happened afterward that I bumped into that very girl in the hallway, and dared to strike up a conversation. Now, nearly fifty years later, it just so happens we're still married.

How many incidents each day do we write off as random happenstance, when God is constructing countless new narratives in the lives of people around us? There are redemptive stories working to their climax in every direction. Many of them we'll never hear, but it doesn't mean God isn't endlessly re-creating, endlessly bringing hope from despair and new life from death. What is it he is quietly doing in your life right now?

This is a powerful truth for those who are struggling in family situations. Why does God allow this pain? Perhaps a better question is, *What does God have planned for these pieces of my broken dream?*

If you're struggling right now, expect a few redemptive coincidences, just in the nick of time. And when they arrive, please give God your gratitude and glory.

J. Wallace Hamilton told of a mother cat, with a newborn kitten in her mouth, trying to cross a busy intersection in New York City. The traffic surely terrified her, as she would dart out, then dash back to the curb as another onrushing vehicle came at her. Sooner or later, that cat was going to become impatient and run under the tires of a heedless vehicle.

Finally a traffic cop walked out to the middle and stopped traffic in both directions, allowing the harried mother feline to dart across and into an alley. She was just a cat, after all, and couldn't have realized the forces at work to enable her salvation—the authority of the NYPD. From her perspective, a lot of cars simply halted for no reason.

Joseph couldn't have realized the workings of God as hostile slave traders bore him away from his home. Nor can you understand the spiritual forces at work all around you, even as the universe seems cold and uncaring. Your struggling family isn't the only family you belong to. You're in God's family, and he hasn't turned his back on you. Quite often, the cruelest-seeming developments become the very turning points toward some new and wonderful divine initiative.

Sometimes the canvas is so large we couldn't begin to imagine what God has in mind. The recent film *Lincoln* showed a president's marriage in turmoil, and history bears out the observation. Gary Thomas, in his book *Sacred Marriage,* suggests that as the president struggled to keep his home together, the result was that he was wiser and more courageous in keeping his nation together.

God wants every family to be a winner, but even when that can't be the case, he is certainly working through the turmoil toward some other marvelous purpose.

DIFFERENCE MAKERS

We label many incidents as "coincidences," when in fact they are part of God's agenda. God is always at work. Another truth we need to underline is that, while it's difficult to come through a troubled home with grace, it's not impossible.

As I've shown, I had one football teammate whose life never escaped the spiral of frustration and error; another who knew how to use his pain and grow from it, so that every tear became water in the soil of a new and wonderful future God was planting for him. The Lord wants that for all of us—but can we see it? Can we take hold of the guidance he wants to give us?

As I thought about these difficult issues, I realized I needed to hear from people who had endured the pain of family dysfunction and come through it in spiritual health. I spoke to an acquaintance whose father sexually abused her in childhood. I can't imagine a darker beginning in life than that. Yet today she's a loving wife, a godly mother, and a wise counselor. No one would guess the darkness of her beginnings in life. I asked her what made the difference. How did she overcome what was taken from her?

It was clear to me she'd given those questions a lot of thought, because she offered me a list of factors that helped her overcome the misfortunes of her childhood. She has given me permission to share her list with you.

1. I spent time each night alone with God. With a sense of his presence, I prayed, read my Bible—the Proverbs were particularly helpful—I journaled, and I shed a few tears.
2. I made our church the center of my social life.
3. I chose to attend a Christian college in a small town.
4. I made sure I knew how to support myself, so that moving back home would never be my only option.

5. For six months I attended weekly Christian counseling, and I took the guidance seriously. Whatever I was asked to do, I did. I was quick to accept counseling whenever I needed it.
6. I read. Specifically, I read Christian books. Since I needed models of marriage and parenting, these volumes changed my outlook. I heard from many wise minds.
7. I attended a ladies' Bible study.
8. I was constantly on the lookout for positive role models and mentors.
9. I married the best man I could find!
10. I learned to honor him.
11. I determined early on to live far away from my family of origin.
12. This was difficult at first, but I never left my kids in the care of my parents.
13. I determined to live a life of honesty, to be an open book with others, free of secrets.
14. I did my very best to grieve what was lost and honor what was still good. I cherished the good in life.
15. I asked God to bless my obedience and faith as I break the cycle of generational sin.

This woman made every right choice, don't you think? I would describe her response to what she suffered as an aggressive initiative against the legacy of evil. Sometimes I think people forget that we have the ability to take action in our plight; to fight back, using godly weapons. That's exactly what she did. So much of God's grace is available for those willing to break life's tragic cycles. He has left a world of redemptive options open to us, beginning with the unlimited power of his indwelling Spirit. Beyond that, there are good people to comfort and guide us. There are good habits to place us on new footing. There are good books, good counseling options, and good decisions that we can make every day.

If I were emerging from the kind of abuse my friend did, I would sit down, with the help of wise believers, and make an action list something like the one above. The simple act of prayerfully writing it down would fill me with a sense of purpose and resolve. Then I would keep that list in a place where I would see it and be reminded of it every day. I'd have a close, trusted friend hold me accountable to continuing in the right directions. And then I would take on my life, one day at a time, with a huge emphasis on the power of God's future over the devil's past.

THE PRESS-ON PRINCIPLE

On the other hand, I can imagine someone reading the last paragraph and saying, "Pastor, it sounds fine and good if you're in the frame of mind to be that positive. But that's the problem. I'm hurting so much that every last ounce of hope seems to have drained out of me. I'm asked to trust in God's love when I can't even love myself, so how am I supposed to experience these blessings? It's hard to comprehend the damage unless you've been there."

I would understand, because I've counseled so many people over the years who feel just that way. Even so, I can say that if you can't feel the reality of God right now, it doesn't mean it's not there. It only means there's an *urgency* for you to feel his love. He is the only true healer, and he knows the pain you feel; he's eager to get into your life and do a miraculous work of restoration. And he is reaching out to you even now; you only need to be open and receptive. So I would plead with you, even if you don't particularly feel like it; even if you're weeping; even if you feel utterly empty of faith and on the doorstep of despair—I would plead with you to ask God to make his healing love real to you.

> **I WOULD** plead with you to ask God to make his healing love real to you.

First, ask him to help you see yourself as *he* sees you, rather than the

HE KNOWS about your pain, but what he sees is what you *can* be.

way you've been made to feel. You are a new creation in Christ, even if it feels precisely the opposite. Because of the work of Christ, sin and death ultimately have no power over you. That means that yes, you can feel the effects of sin in daily life, but Christ has overcome it, so that on a daily basis, you can too, with his guidance.

It also means that when God looks at you, he doesn't see the damage and the sin; he sees the purity and beauty of his own Son, who exchanged his perfection for all our sinful baggage. Resurrection isn't simply something that happens after we die; it's for this very moment. Redemption begins right now.

We are invited to rise and walk, like the wounded individuals Jesus so often healed during his years of physical ministry. He knows about your pain, but what he sees is what you *can* be—what he designed you to be—a beautiful, gifted child of God, consumed with joy and service.

Next, ask him for something truly challenging. Ask him to help you *forgive*. For some, this seems impossible—*how can I forgive a person who did this thing to me?*

It could be the parent who failed you. If you're a parent, it could be the child who rebelled. If you've been married, it could be the spouse who betrayed and left you. Forgiveness is a choice, it's an act of courage, and, for healing truly to be accomplished, it requires the grace and power of God.

I want you to understand that it's profoundly important to forgive for a number of reasons, but one of the most important is that, as long as you hold on to bitterness, you yourself can never heal. Bitterness is an insidious, parasitic entity that takes ever greater power over its host. It poisons every kind of thought we have. It's not so much a question of the other person needing your forgiveness—though that may be true. It's a matter of you needing to forgive for the sake of your spiritual and emotional health.

As you ask God to grant you such powerful grace, ask him to help you move away from your past. It could be that professional counseling could help you do that; in any case, God can. There is a time and a season for facing and acknowledging the past, and a time and a season for moving on. I've talked to people who allow the past to keep haunting them, so that they're hardly aware of the present and all the wonderful realities it holds.

In his letter to the Philippians, Paul speaks twice of "pressing on"—aggressively, proactively pushing forward to take hold of that for which Christ took hold of him. He knows he hasn't arrived. But the point is he is on the move! He is going somewhere:

> *Brothers and sisters, I do not consider myself yet to have taken hold of it. But one thing I do: Forgetting what is behind and straining toward what is ahead, I press on toward the goal to win the prize for which God has called me heavenward in Christ Jesus.*
> —Philippians 3:13–14

Note how dynamic his language is. He is *straining* toward a future of blessing he knows God has prepared for him. Like an athlete, he is determined to *win the prize.* His direction? *Heavenward.*

Action is a medicine unto itself, but particularly when it has a godly context. When Joseph became a slave, as we'll see, there were limits to just how much action he could take. He was now a piece of property. And yet he did his work so well, and exhibited such a positive approach to life, that he moved quickly through the ranks. What the brothers did was solidly in his rearview mirror, and he was moving on, even as a slave in a foreign country. Eventually he became Egypt's deputy Pharaoh—the second most powerful man in the world's most powerful nation of that time.

That's a long way from the deep hole in which Joseph's brothers left him. Whatever your pain may be, it can't reach any deeper than the miracle he has in mind for you.

In Christ, there are no limits. It's simply up to your ability to take hold of that for which he has taken hold of you. *Press on.*

CYCLE BREAKERS

I think you can see the big issue we've raised in these chapters. Sin is plenty terrible enough for what it does here and now. But the vicious cycle it creates multiplies the tragedy. Damaged children are too likely to become damaged parents. If you go out today and sin against a friend, he may, in anger, sin against someone else. And on it goes. As we've said, sin has a viral element to it. It begets more sin, unless something—*someone*—breaks the cycle.

The question, then, is can you be a cycle breaker? Joseph was one. One of my two teammates broke the cycle, while the other did not. My female friend in this chapter did it.

Another cycle breaker was my father, who grew up in a dreadful home. He was the seventeenth of eighteen children, and his mother died when he was three. His father was a coal miner who struggled with both alcohol and women. He had been raised by older sisters who had their own issues. His was a nonbelieving, dysfunctional family environment.

Then something happened that changed his destiny.

In his early twenties, Charles Russell met Catherine Pratt. She was a woman with a deep and abiding love for Jesus Christ. He had never seen a force as powerful and all-defining as the faith she carried with her. No one else was like her. And he wanted that faith the way he wanted her. She led him to the living water, and with work and love and life, the cycle was broken. He followed Christ far away from the heartbreak of his past, each day putting more distance between himself and his beginning.

Sometimes I wonder what would have happened if Catherine Pratt had not led my father to the Lord, but I had been born to them anyway. What kind of home would I have inherited? What would I be like now? Thanks be to God, I'll never know the answer to those questions. I had the privilege of growing up in a loving, harmonious, Christ-centered home.

You can do that. You are not defined by the pieces of a broken heart—not when a brand-new heart is available. You can break the cycle, raise a wonderful family, and live to see your children rise up to call you blessed.

I also think of Jesus, who, at some point, lost his earthly father. After the temple visit in Jesus' twelfth year, Joseph disappears from the Gospels. At the cross, Mary, his mother, is present, but not Joseph. The assumption has always been that Joseph died sometime during those years between twelve and about thirty, during which nothing is known of Jesus' life.

What we do know is that the day came when He heard the voice of his heavenly Father saying, "This is My beloved Son, in whom I am well pleased" (Matthew 3:17 NKJV).

I know he missed the good man, the carpenter who brought him up, sheltered him, and protected Him from evil. Yet what made the difference in his life was another Father, one who can never be lost, one who will never disappoint us or forsake us. And what he said about Jesus, he will say about you and me. We are beloved. In us, he is well pleased.

ACTS OF GOD IN THE FAMILY

As we conclude this issue of family dysfunction, we must ask again: *Why?* What is God up to in allowing the terrible pain that exists in so many families? It's a bit too easy to wave a dismissive hand and say, "Well, all things work together. This too shall pass. God has his purposes."

He *does* have his purposes. He *is* at work, even in the darkest moments of life. But we can't corner the market on answers to the mysteries of suffering in the world. At some point it has to be enough that he is there, that he cares, and that he offers us an opportunity to turn ashes to gold. And like the mountain climber, we have to keep looking up, realizing that the highest moments are yet ahead. We've already used the illustration of climbing Mt. Everest. Interestingly, I found another use of that singular experience as a metaphor for families.

Terry Orlick and Shaunia Burke, a pair of sports psychologists, were intrigued by the select list of individuals who had made it to the summit of Everest. They interviewed a number of them and asked them what it took to achieve the goal. One of them said that he found it essential in life to experience hardship.

> "I've suffered a lot on other expeditions before going to Everest," he said. "People often asked me what it takes to do Everest, and to be honest, it is a lifetime of suffering. That is what you draw on, that ability to say, 'I can sustain the suffering.' Climbing Everest is like an aching tiredness that goes right into the depths of your soul. So the first time hardship shows up on Everest—and it is a very long suffering period—you are able to endure because you say, 'Yes, I have suffered like this before and I have suffered for protracted periods of time.'" [4]

As we've discussed in earlier chapters, suffering should always be seen, along with all that is difficult about it, as a source of new strength. No, it's not a good thing in itself. But it's a thing that, in the hands of God, builds stronger human beings. The steady upward climb of life is demanding, and it won't be made by pampered children. It couldn't have been made by Joseph unless he first learned to trust God in the midst of pain.

The family is a human cocoon. As you know, the homely little caterpillar enters a season of life in which he builds a little compartment and vanishes into it for a while. It's sticky, protective, and a natural laboratory for the butterfly that is going to emerge. But I heard about a little boy who was captivated by coming across a cocoon. He could see the opaque form of a creature struggling to emerge. Being a good-hearted boy, he wanted to help. He tore open the sticky strands and smiled to see the wet fledgling butterfly that emerged.

But it didn't flit away with beautiful wings. It tried, but it quickly and feebly fell to the earth, gasping for breath. The boy was upset, and he told his parents about the experience that evening over dinner. They hugged him and explained that he had learned an important lesson. Nature is sacred. It has its own systems, and they must be respected. The caterpillar must build his muscles—muscles just now forming—if he is going to fly away safely. The cocoon is the instrument by which he gains strength, and that takes fighting his way out of the cocoon.

The family is not meant to be a sticky situation. It shouldn't be a struggle for life. But sometimes we do have to fight our way through its problems. If not there, we'll have to do it somewhere else. The fact is that suffering is God's laboratory for character-building. One of the wisest ways to get through it is to realize that God is on the move. He isn't causing your struggling, but he is making good use of it for a future you can't see.

And the darker a night is, the brighter the morning will seem once it dawns. Then you'll walk forward into the rich, exciting future God has for you, filled with his grace and his brilliant intentions for you.

On that day, as the cycle is broken, he'll turn your tears to laughter. He has a way of doing that.

QUESTIONS FOR YOU

1. Who do you know who endured a dysfunctional child-hood? How would you evaluate the way it affected their adult life?

2. What are some factors that contributed to Jacob's mishandling of the rift between Joseph and his brothers?

3. What is the generational problem, or vicious cycle, of sin? How can the cycle be broken?

4. What is the most personally crucial reason to forgive someone else?

5. Discuss the prescription for surviving family problems that you found most powerful in this chapter—and how you'll put it into practice.

5: TRIALS AND TEMPTATIONS

Where Is God When the Enemy Attacks?

HIS CAREER MADE HIM one of the most respected and admired men in the world; a four-star general, and a major architect of the American war effort in Iraq and Afghanistan.

He served under two administrations, one from each political party. In an era of political division, he was that rare example of public servant about whom all could agree: His work was outstanding.

He was just the man to be appointed as director of the Central Intelligence Agency, a post requiring a leader with a powerful and spotless reputation. He led the CIA for one year until scandal brought him down and, in one fell swoop, destroyed all that he had worked for in a distinguished career.

News broke of an extramarital affair—a simple failure of discipline at the most basic level. How does that happen in the life of a man who followed the intense personal discipline of the military for so long? He had been married for thirty-seven years.

"Such behavior is unacceptable, both as a husband and as the leader of an organization such as ours," said this very public figure in his public statement.

Like Esau from the Bible—Joseph's uncle—he sold his birthright for the cheap, momentary cravings of physical appetite. It made no sense from a rational perspective, yet we've seen it all before, too many times.

We've watched as pastors and presidents, generals and gentlemen squandered their reputations because of a tragic misjudgment.

We can only imagine that it was the work of a weak, unguarded moment when a good but imperfect man did the easy thing rather than the right one.

That's how temptation works. It pursues us, probing and prodding until it finds the right lure at the most vulnerable moment. It only takes once. And then we take some action that can never be taken back or undone, no matter how deep and painful our regrets may be. Temptation does its work, sin closes the deal, and the damage is done.

I believe we take this issue all too lightly in today's world. We make plenty of jokes about it. "Lead me not into temptation," says one slogan. "I already know the way." Oscar Wilde famously made the flippant remark, "I can avoid anything except temptation." When he made the remark, he was at the height of his fame as a literary figure. Later, he was imprisoned for gross immorality, and he died in jail, miserable and humiliated.

Giving in to temptation is something we treat as a stumble, a misstep, something to laugh over. But it can be defined as sin's subtle request to come into our life for a visit. And sin is the type of guest that always outstays its welcome.

SMALL compromises lead to great failures.

When we give in to temptation, the result can be a large and public failing, such as the one we've just discussed; or it can be a small and private one—the furtive cigarette by the one trying to stop smoking; the quick glance at computer pornography by the businessman who tells himself, "No one will know."

But that's not correct, is it? God knows. And *we* know—we know we've given in, we know we were weak, and the next time it will be just a little easier to fail once more.

The devil says, "No one will know." He says, "It's just a little thing." He says, "Just this once." He tells you, "Don't sweat the small stuff—and hey, it's *all* small stuff." But that's not correct either. Small compromises lead to great failures. And you wake up one day to find yourself in shackles too thick to break.

The truth is that every temptation is a more profound spiritual encounter than we realize. Let's explore why that is.

THE BAIT AND THE BITE

We're discussing acts of God and the reactions of people. Is temptation an act of God? No, though some people get that idea. They feel the pull of unhealthy desires, and they feel guilty about thoughts they don't want to have. But James helps us to understand exactly what the connection between temptation and sin is:

> *When tempted, no one should say, "God is tempting me." For God cannot be tempted by evil, nor does he tempt anyone; but each person is tempted when they are dragged away by their own evil desire and enticed. Then, after desire has conceived, it gives birth to sin; and sin, when it is full-grown, gives birth to death.*
>
> —James 1:13–15

Temptation itself is not an act of God. Instead, it's the sad result of our fallen state. Ever since Adam and Eve gave in to that very first temptation, their failure is our failure. The serpent returns with whatever forbidden fruit he believes will get our attention.

James uses the language of fishermen in his description: "dragged away" and "enticed," in his original language, are terms that described how a fish might be lured from shelter at the sight of bait. Enticement is the work of our own appetite, which causes us to throw caution to the wind and satisfy an urge. Temptation is a fishing expedition, and we're the prey.

The Eskimos trap wolves using the same idea. They dip their knives in animal blood, then push the handle into the ground so that the blade points at the sky. Wolves smell the blood and come running to lick at the knife. The frenzy of feeding causes the wolf to lick harder and harder to get every drop. But what about the pain? Appetite keeps the wolf from even noticing the wounds he is self-inflicting. Next day, the hunter casually walks up and collects his quarry.

God did create appetite. But every good gift he gave us can be misused. When our cravings take control, we can do things that have nothing to do with reason. We want what we want, and we don't realize how deep that knife cuts. By the time we do, it's too late to stop the bleeding.

What tempts you? As you read this chapter, I hope you'll keep your personal application in the forefront of your mind, because the devil's strategies never change. We live in a world filled with every kind of temptation. No matter what your "thing" is, someone wants to use it for your destruction.

It's time for us to take temptation seriously and realize that it's the enemy of a healthy spirit.

TEMPTED IN AMERICA

America is a land of prosperity, and therefore a land of temptation. But what tempts people in the United States? A 2011 survey sounded people out on that question. Here are the top answers:

- Worrying or being anxious—60 percent
- Procrastinating or putting things off—60 percent
- Eating too much—55 percent
- Spending too much time on media—44 percent
- Being lazy—41 percent
- Spending more money than they could afford—35 percent

- Gossiping about others—26 percent
- Being jealous or envious of others—24 percent
- Viewing pornography or sexually explicit material—18 percent
- Abusing alcohol or drugs—11 percent

Do Americans have a plan for fighting temptation? When asked if they do anything specific to beat it, 41 percent said yes and 59 percent said no.

Other than not having a plan, why do people give in? Top four answers:

- I am not really sure—50 percent
- To escape or get away from "real life"—20 percent
- To feel less pain or loneliness—8 percent
- To satisfy other people's expectations—7 percent

Source: Todd Hunter, *Our Favorite Sins* (Nashville, TN: Thomas Nelson, 2012), 237–45.

WORK LIKE AN EGYPTIAN

Meanwhile, somewhere on the Mediterranean Highway, in the southbound lane . . .

Joseph must have been feeling as if God was finished with him— and why would that possibly be? Hadn't he been having dreams of grandeur, visions of great things God was going to do in his life? And now, all of a sudden, his brothers had turned on him and sold him into slavery to merchants who would deal him away to Egypt.

Sure, he could have been murdered. He'd heard them seriously discussing that option. Perhaps he was lucky to be alive, but who would be counting their blessings now? At seventeen, a pampered rich boy was facing a lifetime of heavy lifting, the prospect of being another man's property.

Life can turn inside out in the flicker of a moment. One minute everything is right with the world, and life makes sense. The next, you suddenly have no job. Or your spouse announces that your marriage is over. Or there's a shocking report from the doctor.

How do you handle crisis moments, when life takes a left turn? It's not the sunny seasons of life that reveal our inner strength, but the storms. It's so often a dividing point for faith: You either turn from God in anger, believing he has abandoned you; or you reach for a tighter grip on his hand, knowing that you cannot and will not weather this storm without him.

> **FOR THE** first time in his life, Joseph did something impressive: He trusted in God's light when his whole world had gone dark.

For the first time in his life, Joseph did something impressive: He trusted in God's light when his whole world had gone dark. Having done this, ironically enough, he actually confirmed what his dreams had insisted about him. Yes, this would be a man of strength and leadership after all.

Forget the youthful arrogance, the chip on the shoulder. Deep inside this young man was a faith built to last. For now, when anger or self-pity might have gotten its grip into him, he found the strength to make the best of his situation. He simply bloomed in the foreign desert soil in which he had been planted.

Wise followers of Christ know that God wastes nothing. Wherever they are, the Lord has something for them to do. Therefore they don't "wait for their ship to come in." They start building a dock. Consider the case of Steve Prohm, whose dream was to be a basketball coach. Of course, lots of people share that dream of making their favorite sport into a career. Things weren't working out for Steve. He ended up as a clerk in a Blockbuster video store. It was the only way he could provide for his basic needs.

One day Steve was on a ladder, replacing a burned-out light, when the new bulb slipped out of his hands and shattered on the floor. As he sighed and stepped down to clean up the mess, he must have been thinking, *There's my career for you—moving right down the ladder instead of up. Trying to make the light come on, but only making a big mess.*

An aisle or two away, a father was watching all this. He nudged his son and said, "That's why you need to go to college, son. So you don't wind up like that guy, doing odd jobs in a Blockbuster."

Steve overheard, and the words were piercing. But he kept on plugging. And a few months later, an acquaintance got a job coaching basketball at Centenary College and invited Steve to join his staff as a volunteer. Steve was determined to follow his dream and immediately accepted the position. The coach, Billy Kennedy, was soon impressed with Steve's knowledge of the game and his work ethic. A few years later Stove Prohm wound up as Kennedy's assistant at Murray State University in Kentucky.

Steve performed his job with excellence. Everyone was impressed with the way he worked with people, the way he recruited, the positive attitude with which he carried himself. A few years later when Billy Kennedy moved on to another position, Steve was appointed the head man at Murray. He had impressed so many people around him that he was promoted to head coach.

During his first season, Murray State had one of its greatest years ever. The small, unheralded school was in the NCAA Top Ten all year, and made an impressive run during tournament time. March Madness? Steve's march toward success wasn't madness at all. It was a modern-day Joseph story, a case study of what happens when we're willing to bloom where we're planted.

THE BLESSING FACTOR

How did Joseph create such a turnaround?

He had been sold to the household of one Potiphar, a high government official of the Pharaoh. As a new slave—a teenage one who had barely lifted a hand in labor—Joseph would have started at the very bottom of the heap. He didn't know the language or the customs. He wasn't exactly capable of heavy lifting. We can assume he carried trash, cleaned up after others, and caught the worst even from the other slaves.

And yet Joseph found his niche, proved himself, and began to catch the attention of his masters. Whatever he did, he excelled at it. People liked him. Ten years passed, and he found himself running Potiphar's household. He had become something more than a slave—he was a right-hand assistant. It's one thing to give the keys of your business to someone; to let him run your home implies a far deeper level of confidence. Joseph had come a long way.

HOW OFTEN do we realize that our obedience brings the blessing of God to others?

Something else was going on, too—something visible only to the spiritually discerning:

> *From the time he put him in charge of his household and of all that he owned, the LORD blessed the household of the Egyptian because of Joseph. The blessing of the LORD was on everything Potiphar had, both in the house and in the field.*
>
> —Genesis 39:5

Had God abandoned Joseph? On the contrary, the Bible tells us that God was in control all along. It was God who saw that Joseph ended up where he did. It was God who blessed this one household *because of Joseph.*

How often do we realize that our obedience brings the blessing of God to others? It's easier to understand how our disobedience curses many other lives. But when a man or woman loves and serves God, that person creates a kind of blessing zone that enriches others. Potiphar knew a good thing when he saw it, and the Bible tells us, in the next verse, that the dignitary made no decisions in his own household other than what to eat for his next meal. He trusted Joseph completely for everything, and as a result, he shared in the blessings of Joseph's relationship with God.

And that brought a time of testing.

Yes, just when things were going so well—God permitted Joseph to be tested. Let's think about why.

TEST TIME

Think of your school years. It was a long, steady path from one educational level to the next higher one, punctuated by a stressful series of tests and examinations. To get to the next grade, you had to be tested and show that you were proficient at the present one. That required studying, learning, and preparation. Then, when you passed, you knew you had achieved something worthwhile.

Spiritual growth works the same way. You're always moving toward a new position of maturity, but there are tests along the way. How you handle them shows how far you've come. Tests are necessary, for they get our full attention. They force us to make decisions. They build character and wisdom, and they're part of God's plan for conforming us to the image of his Son.

There's a crucial distinction here. We've seen that God tempts no one. On the other hand, he *tests* everyone. Testing is a way of building us up, while tempting is a way of breaking us down. If you are being tested right now, be encouraged! While no one likes difficult challenges, it's good to know that God is moving us toward the next level.

Again, we listen to the counsel of James:

> *Blessed is the one who perseveres under trial because, having stood the test, that person will receive the crown of life that the Lord has promised to those who love him.*
>
> —James 1:12

Joseph had passed the ten-year test of faith, with the highest score. Now it was time for a more difficult examination, over in the Sexual Morality department. His spirit had come through, but now would come a test of his flesh.

We read that Joseph had matured into an impressive young man during this period. Now about twenty-seven, he was strong, handsome, and self-confident. It's no surprise that the devil made this choice. Lust is one of his old, reliable lures. And it would have also pleased Joseph's vanity to be found desirable by the wife of his master. That's exactly what happened: Potiphar's wife began watching him. We've already been told that her husband was inattentive to the household, and that made it easy for her to be attentive to Joseph.

One day, she came sidling up to him, offered him her smoothest smile, and invited him to her bed.

Joseph did well on the first part of the test. He respectfully declined the invitation, telling her that his master trusted him; that her husband had put him in a position of high responsibility. He said,

> *No one is greater in this house than I am. My master has withheld nothing from me except you, because you are his wife. How then could I do such a wicked thing and sin against God?*
>
> —Genesis 39:9

See how Joseph explains his responsibilities to *two* masters. Obviously there is Potiphar. But then he asks how he could ever commit a "sin against God." Joseph understands what is really at stake here. Underneath every sin we commit against each other lies a sin against God himself. All of us serve two masters.

God has taken care of Joseph all his life, and particularly during ten years of slavery. The young man might have been dead by now, but life has gone well. God has honored Joseph—could Joseph even consider dishonoring God?

Notice what this means for facing temptation. Here is a moment when lust could take over. If he thought the way people often do today, he could have told himself, "I've worked hard. I've got some *me* time coming to me." Instead, he is able to think clearly—to sort out the honor and trust issues (Potiphar) and the spiritual issues (God).

Clear thinking always helps us on a test, doesn't it? The greatest danger of temptation is that our appetites dull our judgment, much like the Alaskan wolf. We need to be as sharp and spiritually vigilant in our thinking as Joseph was.

Joseph has done well, but it's too early for celebrations. This test is multiple choice—that is, each day, Joseph has to make the choice again, as Potiphar's wife renews her pursuit. Everyone who has ever been on a diet or an exercise program knows that life is tough because it's so *daily*. It's easy to ace the first day of a diet or an exercise plan. But can you do it again tomorrow? What about two weeks after that? Standing firm against temptation isn't a sprint but a marathon. It requires commitment to God, self-discipline, and perseverance.

Before we find out what happens next in Joseph's compelling life, let's explore three key principles in this subject of temptation.

TRUTHS ABOUT TEMPTATION

1. We're fighting a war with eternal consequences.

Have you ever noticed how professional football players play the Super Bowl? They know the whole world is watching. This is the literal endgame for a season of this sport. Nobody gives half-effort. Everything is on the line, and the emotions are intense; the focus is laser-quality. And with a global grandstand, even the commercials cost millions of dollars and are scrutinized the next day.

The moment of temptation is a Super Bowl moment for you. Don't buy into the idea that this is no big deal, and that nobody is watching. "For our struggle is not against flesh and blood, but against the rulers, against the authorities, against the powers of this dark world and against the spiritual forces of evil in the heavenly realms" (Ephesians 6:12).

The Roman general in the film *Gladiator* offered his own version of Paul's passage: "What we do in life echoes in eternity." You are an eternal creature, a soul precious to God. He is eager for you to be moving forward toward your transformation to the amazing person he has planned you to be. Each test has the opportunity to bring you one step closer to being conformed to the image of Christ. It also provides the danger that you fail, slipping further from that goal.

The devil lays his traps, but God always provides the strength to help us avoid them. He did that for Joseph, and he'll do that for you.

2. We're suffering higher casualties as the enemy intensifies his attack.

Jesus taught his disciples about the last days, and he made it very clear that the world would become an increasingly ugly place before he returned. There would be a spike in cultural wickedness; the love of many would grow cold (Matthew 24:12). The devil's own endgame is similar to what happens in any national conflict. As wars fight down to the bitter end, a cornered enemy drops all pretense of fighting fairly, and he resorts to every kind of dirty tactic.

The devil understands that his days grow shorter. It's a war he has already lost, but there are still individual skirmishes he can win. We are actually seeing him invent new kinds of evil. A few decades ago, we couldn't have imagined Internet pornography that children can access. We've seen horrific methods of mass destruction, such as airplanes used as lethal weapons. We've seen the suppression of truth in academic and media circles.

The enemy, then, is opening up new fronts. He is particularly targeting our spiritual leaders. I participated in a sermon study group for a decade, and two of the pastors with whom I worked recently confessed to extramarital affairs. Both of them ministered to churches with more than one thousand attenders. Their churches were traumatized; the two families were devastated. In one case, the pastor's family broke up. Friends and relatives were hurt. This is the kind of "skirmish" the devil uses to his advantage.

But even then, God has the power and the grace to turn tragedy to victory. We need to reach out and nurture those who have fallen, helping them on their paths of repentance and restoration. Yet diversionary tactics by Satan continue. We end up focusing inward, to our own problems in the church, rather than outward, where the ultimate battle is. It would certainly be to our advantage to win out over temptation in the first place, rather than spending our time picking up the pieces.

We'd better be prepared for this fight, because the enemy certainly is.

3. We have points of vulnerability and we need to fortify ourselves.

During the Iraqi War, Secretary of Defense Donald Rumsfeld traveled to Kuwait to encourage the troops at one of the US bases. As he was speaking to the troops, he received a question he found difficult to answer, and it quickly led to a public debate back in the United States.

Army Specialist Thomas Wilson of the 278th Regimental Combat Team stepped up and asked, "Why do we soldiers have to dig through local landfills for pieces of scrap metal and compromised ballistic glass to up-armor our vehicles?"[5]

In layman's terms, he was asking why our soldiers were being sent into harm's way with insufficient protection. Our troops were serving courageously, yet living each moment with the knowledge that a hidden bomb or a sniper's bullet could come from nowhere. It was time for us to do a better job of protecting our warriors.

Spiritually, it makes no sense to go into battle without the best protection available. Yet that's how many of us live our lives. Paul wrote about "the flaming arrows of the evil one," and pointed out that "the shield of faith" neutralizes them (Ephesians 6:16).

We can't afford to go into battle unprepared. Let's examine the devil's three-pronged attack.

THE WORLD, THE FLESH, AND THE DEVIL

The devil attacks from every angle, using temptation as the supreme weapon in his arsenal. He targets our points of vulnerability. The Bible teaches that the three sources of enemy fire are the world, the flesh, and the devil himself.

The world refers to the organized social system in which we live. Peer pressure is powerful, and when we're surrounded by people who are constantly retreating in their opposition to evil, our own morale suffers. Why should we be the only ones who still speak out against sexual immorality? Don't God's standards seem a little antiquated to us after we spend a little time with our friends from work? "Bad company corrupts good character" (1 Corinthians 15:33). When you devote too much time to certain poor influences, "you may learn their ways and get yourself ensnared" (Proverbs 22:25). *Ensnared* is, again, a trapping term.

By this term *the world* we mean our community, our media voices, our institutions of government and education and entertainment. All of these influence us, whether we realize it or not. There is *always* a spiritual agenda, because we are created as spiritual people.

The flesh is the Bible's term for the sinful nature we have inherited as human beings. God made eating, but we can overeat. God created sexuality, yet we can abuse that gift, too. The flesh in us is constantly trying to throw us off balance and trip us up. Paul wrote, "For I know that good itself does not dwell in me, that is, in my sinful nature" (Romans 7:18). And we remember the teaching of James, near the beginning of this chapter, showing how our own desires lure and entice us, leading to sin and ultimately death.

If you don't believe we're born in sin, you've never told a two-year-old not to touch something. Children are innately rebellious, and one of the central initiatives of parenting is to teach them discipline and obedience. If babies were born in perfection, they would smile and thank us the first time we changed a diaper.

For a good illustration of our natural tendency toward insubordination, notice how we're commanded not to take God's name in vain. That's a very simple request, isn't it? One name is off limits, countless names from history are available for us to throw around, and yet people can't stay away from misusing the one forbidden name. No one yells, "Jimmy Carter!" when he becomes angry. Nobody creates epithets around the name of Julius Caesar.

Why is this? Because our very natures are in revolt against God and his commands. And even after we become Christians, that flesh nature still pulls at us. You are a new creature in Christ, but the old self still fights for control, and always will during your days on this planet.

The devil himself is not to be forgotten. Ultimately he is the architect of the other side of the war we are fighting; evil's supreme commander. This is why we call him "the prince of this world" (John 12:31). He realizes exactly where our weak spots are, and he lays the snares to capture us.

ACTS OF GOD IN TIMES OF TEMPTATION

God never tempts, but he allows us to be tested and tried. If we will allow it, he'll turn the most vicious attacks of the enemy back against him. What seemed to be curses will be turned to blessings in God's hands, as we take the shield of faith and continue to trust him.

It's built into the principles by which God designed this world. Before the Second World War, the United States was the world's eighteenth-ranked military power, just behind Romania. But after Pearl Harbor was attacked, the country mobilized. It was a time of patriotism in America, with citizens making incredible sacrifices to fight world tyranny. Young men hurried to enlist and to offer their lives to frontline service. Families grew "victory gardens" and learned to substitute for rationed supplies of meat, gasoline, and other commodities needed in the war effort.

You could say our country's resolve was tried and tested, and by the time the war was over, the United States stood as a superpower on the international scene. The soldiers came home to build a thriving economy during the following generation. Would America have ever attained its dominance and power as a culture without the tough times of the 1940s? Testing, when handled with maturity, produces outstanding results.

Temptation, however, is going to be a constant companion as long as you live in this world. You can become the wisest and most devoted believer of Jesus Christ, and you'll still cope with the constant probing and prodding of the world, the flesh, and the devil. As you pass test after test, you'll reach higher levels of maturity, bringing tougher forms of testing. You'll be tempted by Satan, tested and tried by God.

But don't be discouraged. You'll be growing stronger during this time, too. Every victory will make it just a little bit easier to prevail the next time. As Potiphar's wife kept after Joseph, we know she never wore him down. The first moment of temptation was surely difficult, but the moments kept coming. After he stood firm, and acknowledged he would not sin against God, he surely knew he could hold out. After that, he grew stronger and stronger, even realizing, in all probability, that the woman would get her revenge.

Throughout the story of Joseph, he is tested in various ways and only becomes a greater man, a more devoted servant of God. That's no coincidence. It's crucial to God's plan for making us what he wants us to be. Have you noticed that the first chapter of James seems to be a commentary on the life of Joseph? Here's how James sums it up:

Blessed is the one who perseveres under trial because, having stood the test, that person will receive the crown of life that the Lord has promised to those who love him.

—James 1:12

That crown of life was, in first-century times, a laurel wreath that was placed on the head of an athletic champion. He had tested his physical limits. He had been tried against the toughest competition. Now he stood in the winner's circle, and the symbol of victory was placed upon his brow. This would ultimately happen in the life of Joseph—though not yet. Joseph had to walk in faith, even in the dark times that would come to him, that God had promised a reward to those who loved him. He had been tempted by the flesh, and had stood firm. He had been tested in his faith, and he grew.

There had been a time when Joseph's "crown of life" was a special robe, given him by his father. That gift crowned nothing but youthful immaturity, and it brought him only grief. It ended up drenched in blood.

We need to remember that the crown God promises us is one of the spirit. His rewards are gifts like wisdom, maturity, patience, strength, faith, hope, and love. None of these can money buy; all are more precious than anything the world could give us.

If you're being tempted now, know that you're also being tested. Temptation is an act of the enemy, who would like to disrupt and destroy your life. But all the while, there is always an ongoing act of God, the miracle that God is performing in you, conforming you to the image of his Son. What will make the difference is how you respond, how you stand in the face of temptation.

In the next chapter, we'll talk about defenses.

QUESTIONS FOR YOU

1. What is the prevalent temptation in your life? What's your strategy for facing it?

2. What are the key differences between temptation and testing? What does God have to do with each?

3. What factors do you think would have made Joseph's temptation in Potiphar's house particularly difficult?

4. What are the differences between the world, the flesh, and the devil? What special powers do each have when it comes to temptation?

5. What practical application from Joseph's experience—and this chapter's discussion—can you best use in your own life?

6: STORM-PROOF

Weathering Life's Dark Moments

MICHAEL P. GHIGLIERI may have written the most disturbing vacation book ever. He decided to study how tourists—nearly 700 of them—have died while visiting the Grand Canyon.

His book *Over the Edge: Death in Grand Canyon* explores all the ways visitors to the great marvel have lost their lives, going back to 1870. Some have died of heatstroke and dehydration. Air crashes have taken a number of lives, and floods have struck, too. Some have committed suicide by jumping over the edge.

But perhaps the most tragic of all have been the lives taken due to nothing but carelessness. A great many deaths could have and should have been prevented. Warning signs are posted in many places, yet something inside people pulls them right up to the edge of the precipice, where terrible things can happen. Call it reckless tragedy.

For example, there was the dad who was joking with his teenage daughter in 1992. He leaped onto a guard wall and flailed his arms, as if he were losing his balance. Then he pretended to fall on the canyon side, where he thought the ledge was safe. But he lost his balance and fell 400 feet to his death.

> **WE DON'T** really believe we're mortal—surely nothing that terrible could happen to you or me.

In 2012, a young lady of eighteen was enjoying her hike when she decided to leave her chosen path and get her picture taken at Inspiration Point. She sat on the ledge, overlooking the 1,500-foot canyon, and rocks came loose. Just like that, she was gone.[6]

We make jokes about "living on the edge." There is some strange impulse that causes people to try to scare each other, or maybe simply capture a quick thrill. We want to go right up to the line of danger, then slide one more toe into the trouble zone. It requires a certain amount of arrogance, doesn't it? We don't really believe we're mortal—surely nothing that terrible could happen to you or me. Except when it finally does.

That's the way it is with temptation. It plays on the human condition, the natural rebelliousness that never totally leaves us. We are moths drawn to the flame.

Just come closer, take a look—I dare you! The hiker and the teenage girl's dad were casual and joking as they put themselves within inches of certain death. They just weren't being realistic.

But then again, how about us? Do we realize the dangers of the influences we let into our homes? Do we understand what is at stake for our children when we fail to guide them in their choices of friends?

It doesn't even have to involve, say, pornography or substance abuse or any of the "usual suspects" we round up on our list of evils. It could be the temptation to keep eating an unhealthy diet, increasing the chances of heart disease. It could be the temptation to put a little more focus on work and a little less on your marriage, as you and your spouse quietly drift apart. It could be the temptation to let your financial debt slide for one more month, rather than imposing some discipline on your budget.

Someone once said that nobody ever jumps into hell; they just fool around the edge and slip. The problem is the idea that we can "fool around" with certain things. As we saw in the last chapter, our struggle is not against flesh and blood. We're engaged in spiritual warfare, and we must be people of discipline and sound minds.

The strongest man in the Bible, Samson, wasn't strong enough to resist temptation—and it was the death of him.

The greatest hero of the Old Testament, David, wasn't heroic when he gave in to the temptation of adultery, then the temptation to cover it up with murder.

The Bible is filled with individuals who struggled with the traps set out for them. Finally there came a man, the Son of God, who walked into the wilderness for prayer, meditation—and a supreme test. The Gospels tell us how Jesus withstood three basic temptations that would have ruined his mission of destiny, had he given in to them.

But those weren't the only temptations he ever faced. For him as for us, being tempted was a daily part of life. Finally, in a garden, he wrestled with the temptation to avoid the cross. How many of us would have finally made the choice he did? Because Jesus was strong in the face of temptation, death itself could be conquered. "For we do not have a high priest who is unable to empathize with our weaknesses, but we have one who has been tempted in every way, just as we are—yet he did not sin" (Hebrews 4:15).

Unlike the Starship Enterprise, we are not going where no man has gone before. No matter what temptation we face—Jesus has been there.

JOSEPH'S TOP TEN

In the prime of his life, Joseph was finding that, against all odds, things were working out. Yes, he was a slave, but he couldn't have felt much like one. He had been entrusted with the home of one of the most powerful men in Egypt. He was a respected leader in his own right. He would have eaten well, been given good clothes, and been on good terms with his master's family.

Those "good terms," however, needed limits. The master's wife came and made a pass at him. It's too easy for us to think of Joseph as larger than life, brushing off the seduction of the moment with ease. Not likely. Let me suggest ten reasons why this was a tough test at a critical time for Joseph:

1. He knew what it was like to be pampered, from his childhood.
2. He was a young man of about twenty-seven, at the height of a man's sexual drive.
3. He knew the loneliness of a servant, single and far from home.
4. He was becoming successful, and power accompanies seduction.
5. He was strong and handsome, and he certainly knew it.
6. His resistance only made him more attractive—more of a challenge.
7. His environment was morally relaxed, compared to his homeland.
8. He was driven and ambitious: to forge this alliance might have solidified his standing, but to insult the boss's wife would be (and was) a career-killer.
9. He had to fend off the advances "day by day." He could have been worn down.
10. He could have kept the affair a secret. Maybe they'd never be caught.

As we've seen, God blessed this home simply because Joseph was in it. Throughout this story, Joseph will go on to bless his various environments, from a dark prison to a bright empire. That's the power of godliness. Our world needs it. We can make a difference when we live by God's laws.

There was a time, recorded in Genesis 18, when Abraham pled for God's mercy on a wicked city that was going to be destroyed. Abraham was asking if God would spare a city for the sake of fifty righteous people. What about forty-five? Thirty? What about ten? The question posed here was: How many godly people does it take for a sinful city to have any hope of avoiding destruction? Sometimes one alone can make a difference. Sometimes it takes a church to save a village.

When you resist temptation, when you stand on integrity, it never occurs in a vacuum. Maybe the people around you will be inspired to do the same. The power of one, in the hands of God, can accomplish great things. The power of a group, standing together, can change the world.

Sadly enough, there isn't enough counsel around us that challenges us to stand firm on godly principles. I can imagine Joseph taking his problem to a modern counselor: "Joe, no one is going to judge you for letting off a little steam, sowing a few wild oats. You've had it hard. You're still dealing with sibling issues. Go and have the fun you've got coming to you. You mention God a lot, but doesn't God want you to be happy?"

Yes, as a matter of fact, God does. But he wants us to have a deep joy, a genuine joy, not the momentary relief of scratching an itch. He wants us to experience the freedom that comes only through obedience, rather than the true slavery that comes from being mastered by our appetites.

As we consider the refusal Joseph offers Potiphar's wife, it's easy for us to forget that Moses and the Ten Commandments were four centuries in the future. Joseph had no law to quote concerning adultery. Such specifics hadn't come down from on high yet. Joseph simply knew in his heart that disloyalty to his master, as well as sexual impurity, were sins against God. We all have that intuition: Paul tells us in Romans 2:15 that the requirements of the law are written on our hearts. He concludes that we are "without excuse" because his truth has been clear to us in creation since the very beginning (Romans 1:18–20).

So God gave Joseph the resources he needed to make the right decision. He does that for you, too.

BOILING POINT

With so many reasons to make the wrong choice, Joseph passed every test. Over time, I believe he only became stronger in his refusal. As we've mentioned, Potiphar's wife would have seen his moral stance as a personal challenge, something to overcome. Day and night, she gave it her best shot. And when it became clear that she couldn't succeed, she took that personally, too. Maybe she had seduced other young men—we can only speculate. But this time her pride was taking a hit. Therefore Joseph had to pay.

One day there was one of those unfortunate moments with no witnesses around. Joseph would have hated those times. Sure enough, on this occasion, Potiphar's wife made a grab at him. Using force where the soft-sell had failed, she seized his cloak and said, "Come to bed with me!" (Genesis 39:12).

Joseph did the brave thing—he fled! There are times when flight isn't cowardly, but the better part of valor. He got himself out of that room, and left the woman with a piece of cloth in her hand. Once again, it was a robe that would get Joseph in trouble. He flaunted one, he fled the other.

Meanwhile, the woman thought quickly. She gathered the other servants and showed them what was in her hand. Then she appealed to their resentment of someone from another land. She told them that this Hebrew had come to make fools of them. He had tried to rape her and fled. She knew what would happen. It would be a slave's word against that of the lady of the house. And no matter what kind of reputation Joseph had compiled, he didn't have the home field in this contest. He was the foreigner. He had to pay.

I'm certain that this woman was all gentle voice and soft caresses while she still believed she could get Joseph into bed. Temptation always wears its best clothing. But once it fails, the masks come off, and we see it for what it really is—something that is no longer using the word *love*, but out to trash the object of pursuit.

When I played football, the coaches would hand out oranges at halftime. They were great thirst-quenchers and energy-replenishers. I would hear guys say, "Man, I *love* oranges." Then they would squeeze the fruit, suck out all the juice until there was nothing but rind, and then toss the remains in the dust.

Sexual temptation says, "I love you." It offers all kinds of words about "how good we are together," how much attraction there is, and how strong the chemistry is between us. But the time comes—either sooner or later—when that person will be discarded like a dried-out rind. That was Potiphar's wife. At some point, she was going to trash him. At least he made sure she did it before he trashed himself.

But was God trashing Joseph? I can imagine it might have felt that way, once he pled innocence and no one believed his story. In all probability, the servants all believed him—but why put their own necks out for this poor guy? He was never a real Egyptian anyway. He had passed them on the hierarchical slave ladder. I can see them all watching quietly, a little smug, as Joseph is arrested for a crime he didn't commit.

One of the times when we question God is the occasion when the right choice brings the wrong result. It's intuitive to us that God should reward—and by "reward," we mean *quickly* reward—the act of integrity. So often that doesn't happen. "Where is your God now?" they asked Jesus on a Friday night, as he bled on a cross. It's not the act of God, but what seems like the inaction, that worries us so.

One of the most important truths of this book is that God's actions happen on God's timetable. We'll begin that conversation in the next chapter. For now, let's realize how it looked to Joseph. He had held out so long, done the right thing, taken his stand—and now he was going to be punished for it.

From Joseph's story we can take several powerful principles for avoiding temptation as it intensifies in our environment.

AN ACTION PLAN

1. Don't be in the wrong place at the wrong time.

It should never happen in church, but of course it does—leaders make disastrous decisions. Because of their kingdom position, they receive more than their share of the enemy's attention.

After a worship leader in our church fell into immorality, I decided to create some very specific guidelines for our staff. They should never ride in a car, go out to eat, or go into a home alone with a member of the opposite sex other than their spouse. We instructed our staff not to have counseling sessions without a third party in the adjacent room.

Such practical steps help avoid bad situations, including accusations or misperceptions, which can be just as destructive even when they're not true. As ambassadors of Christ, not only do we have to avoid evil, but we have to avoid the very appearance of evil. If only a few witnesses had been around, Joseph might have prevented the lies that were told about him. He lost his good name without the sin it should have taken for that to happen.

Joseph was at a disadvantage here, because there weren't many places for him to run and hide. However, the Bible tells us that not only did Joseph refuse to give in to Potiphar's wife, he refused to "even be with her" (Genesis 39:10). That means he tilted the field as much in his favor as possible.

We can avoid a good bit of the problem simply by keeping ourselves away from the place of temptation. A recovering alcoholic finds a new route through town, so that he doesn't have to drive down the road with all the bars and taverns that tempt him. This seems like a no-brainer, but again, as fallen people we have a tendency to want to dance around the edge of the precipice. We deny our own vulnerabilities. We need to take steps to put ourselves out of harm's way.

With the exploding problem of Internet pornography, which is destroying many men's lives, the steps have to be more than geographical.

Some are having special filters installed on their computers so their machines won't even visit certain sites should the users experience a weak moment.

2. Think clearly and biblically.

In the preceding chapter we made this particular observation. Let's review it here. In temptation, our perceptions are often filtered through our appetites—and the result is rationalization. Joseph makes a clear statement of his position before his earthly master and his position before his heavenly one. Genesis 39:8–9 gives us Joseph's words. His final one is that to sleep with this woman would be a "sin against God."

He is thinking *clearly* as he talks about his real-world standing as an employee of Potiphar. He is thinking *biblically* as he talks about the rebellion against God his actions would entail. I wonder how much of a deterrent we could provide simply by adding the word *sin* to our vocabularies during these times. When we're tempted to do something wrong, what if we stopped and asked, *What is this all about? Is this really a reasonable action on my part, or is it good old-fashioned sin? What does Christ, who lives within my heart, think I should do here? What does the Bible say about this kind of activity?*

Clear thinking also means asking ourselves how these actions would affect others. That includes ourselves. *Will this action create a barrier between God and myself when I try to pray?*

3. Ask Jesus Christ to handle it.

Martin Luther, the great Christian reformer from the sixteenth century, had a strong awareness of evil and the work of Satan. At one time, legend has it, he tossed a jar of ink at the wall when he felt the devil harassing him during his writing!

He made a brilliant suggestion for those occasions when we feel the devil knocking at the door of our hearts. Send Jesus to answer it!

In modern words, his prescription would look a little like the following.

You're at home, sitting and thinking, when you hear an automobile pulling into your driveway. You get up and peek through the curtains to see a long, black limousine. You know it well and your heart begins to beat quickly. *Here he comes again,* you think. *Why won't he leave me alone?*

The door of the car opens, and a tall, imposing figure emerges, dressed all in black. As he cuts across your lawn, his feet (are they really feet?) leave scorch-marks in the grass.

Maybe I'll pretend I'm not at home.

No, that won't work. You can feel his eyes burning right through the door, looking at you, smiling . . .

Then the idea comes to you: call upstairs for help!

Outside, the devil continues to knock. "Sooner or later, the door has to come open," he says. You can hear the smirk in his smooth voice. And just then, it does open. But it's not you! It's a man who is even stronger, even more imposing than the visitor. His eyes are unrelenting as he stares down the unwanted guest. The devil gives this figure a good look and sees that the hand on the door is nail-scarred.

"*You?*" asks the devil. "Wait a minute! Isn't this the address of . . ."

"It used to be," says Jesus. "I've moved in now. If you want to deal with my friend, you'll have to go through me from now on."

Soon the car door is slamming, and the limo is screeching away.

This isn't simply an exercise in visualization, or a cute use of the imagination. It's good theology. If you have given your life to Christ, you have identified with him, and he has identified with you—to be precise, he lives within you. he was crucified on your behalf, and the old you was crucified with him. He stands before God, pleading your case; as the old hymn says, your name is written on his hand.

We don't have to fight our battles alone. We can rely on the power of Christ. As Paul describes it:

I have been crucified with Christ and I no longer live, but Christ lives in me. The life I now live in the body, I live by faith in the Son of God, who loved me and gave himself for me.

—Galatians 2:20

When you feel tempted, ask Christ to handle it on your behalf. Call upon his strength to do the right thing.

4. Know when to fight; know when to flee.

The humorist Jack Handey once wrote about the bullies who would push him around on the playground and take his lunch money. He then enrolled in a special program to learn the art of self-defense. After a few lessons, he realized it made more financial sense to just hand over his lunch money to the bully—the lessons cost several times what his lunch money did!

I'm not here to advise anyone to give in to bullies. But when we're talking about temptation, it's not always a good idea to stand and fight. Joseph did the right thing by vacating the premises as soon as Potiphar's wife brought her proposition.

For some of us, the idea of running away doesn't sit right. We have our pride, and our instinct is to resist evil actively. We're instructed, "Resist the devil, and he will flee from you" (James 4:7). That's because he knows when to take flight! When we see evil itself in operation—something where we can make a difference—yes, we should put up resistance in the name of Christ. But temptation is an exception to that. It's a specially arranged attack to the weakest part of our spiritual constitution. Sexual immorality, of course, is one of the highest and most dangerous temptations, so the Bible tells us to "flee from sexual immorality" (1 Corinthians 6:18).

The best resistance we can make is to remove ourselves from the battlefield. It's just a lot less "expensive" in the long run. A reporter asked an African safari guide, "Is it true that ferocious jungle animals won't harm you if you carry a torch?" The guide said, "That depends on how fast you carry it."

There's a poorly conceived idea going around that "strong" Christians don't undergo temptations. Or if they do, they're more than a match for it every time. They simply carry their Bibles and fend off evil. They do—if they carry them fast enough.

Devout, wise believers fail morally all the time. We need to be humble, know our weaknesses, and realize that retreat isn't always surrender.

5. Don't expect quick rewards.

Sometimes we stand firm and get a pat on the back. We walk into a recovery meeting and say, "My name is John Smith and I didn't take a drink all week." Everyone applauds and offers affirmation.

But for the most part, resisting temptation is drudgery, and it doesn't seem to bring any quick rewards. If you really wanted to stop the appetite pangs—whatever kind they may be—you would have given in to your urges. But you knew that wasn't wise. You understood that this was a spiritual issue, an obedience issue. So you said no.

Here's how Joseph was "rewarded" for holding out during a long assault on his sexual morality. Potiphar's wife basically planted evidence, holding on to his cloak. Then she waited for her husband to come home, and she told her sob story. Maybe the servants didn't buy a word of it, assuming they'd been watching Joseph and seeing what kind of person he was. Maybe even Potiphar himself wasn't sure he bought it. He knew both people.

The Bible tells us he "burned with anger." But was all of it focused against Joseph? Could some of it been toward an unreliable wife who cost him his best servant? We can't know that for certain, but it's worth pointing out that Joseph wasn't executed. Surely if a foreign slave truly raped a noblewoman, he would lose his life in that culture. But Joseph was simply sent away to prison. Could it be that nobody really believed the accusations?

This marked the second time in a decade he could have been killed, and wasn't. It brings up this point: Can we see the acts of God when it seems as if he isn't acting at all? Here's what the Bible tells us:

> *The LORD was with him; he showed him kindness and granted him favor in the eyes of the prison warden. So the warden put Joseph in charge of all those held in the prison, and he was made responsible for all that was done there. The warden paid no attention to anything under Joseph's care, because the LORD was with Joseph and gave him success in whatever he did.*
>
> —Genesis 39:21–23

How do we know the Lord was with Joseph, unless Joseph remembered it that way, and bore testimony later to God's kindness? Joseph has a sense of the Lord's presence, even when everything had gone wrong. He understood that ultimately, life is not about quick gratification. The real rewards come from staying the course. That means that suffering will be necessary at times. It means that winning may sometimes feel a lot like losing. Joseph showed tremendous personal discipline, only to be thrown into prison for it.

When we pay the price for doing the right thing, that doesn't mean God is being silent. That's when he is truly acting to do something significant within us. When we come to the point that we can do the hard thing for the right reason, with no hope of reward other than the knowledge of obedience to God, we are drawing within sight of the spiritual destiny he has for us. "Blessed are those who are persecuted because of righteousness, for theirs is the kingdom of heaven" (Matthew 5:10). The real rewards are worth waiting for.

6. Maintain a peaceful spirit.

There are, however, immediate rewards to doing the right thing. One is a peaceful spirit, as well as the maintaining of self-respect.

Bitterness takes a terrible toll on us. Nothing is more corrosive to the spirit than self-pity. But Joseph once again bloomed where he was planted. He was at peace with himself, because he had done no wrong. If he could bloom in the Egyptian sun as a slave, he could do it in the dungeon darkness as an inmate. The same pattern held true—Joseph rose to the highest level of responsibility available to him. You can't keep a good man down.

Remember those dreams he had as a teenager? They seemed arrogant at the time. But God was telling him, "Your destiny is to take charge. It is to lead men." Joseph took hold of that destiny and proved it out, over and over. But he could only prove it out in a context of true accomplishment. Rising through slavery and imprisonment—those are true accomplishments.

Like Joseph, Dietrich Bonhoeffer began life with a silver spoon in his mouth. His family was well off. But before he was forty years old, he was imprisoned due to his failure to support Adolf Hitler. He spent the final eighteen months of his life as a prisoner in a Nazi death camp. Payne Best, another prisoner, described Bonhoeffer as

> all humility and sweetness; he always seemed to me to diffuse an atmosphere of happiness, of joy in every smallest event in life, and of deep gratitude for the mere fact he was alive.... He was one of the very few men that I have ever met of whom his God was real and ever close to him ... he was quite calm and normal, seemingly perfectly at ease ... his soul really shone in the dark desperation of our prison.[7]

Best concluded that Bonhoeffer had always worried that he'd be too weak for the strongest test that God might demand. But now he was spiritually liberated by knowing that, if he could handle this situation, there was nothing else in life he needed to fear.[8]

Bonhoeffer wasn't physically liberated, sadly enough; he died just before the Allied forces could free him. But he won the great prize, the "crown of life" the New Testament describes. His was the kingdom of heaven. We could say the same of Paul, who did his own time in prison and was also executed. His letters show none of the despair of a confined man awaiting his death; they show the joy of another world quickly approaching.

That level of joy, when it shines through the ashes and smog of a difficult world, draws people toward God. An older businessman walked up to me one morning after church, and I smiled and shook his hand. He said, "This is the first time I've gone to church in twenty-five years. I'm here because Bob Drane invited me. You see, he's one of my subcontractors. If there were more Bob Dranes among the people I do business with, my life would be much easier. So when he invites me to church—I'm coming."

MORE WEAPONS FOR THE WARRIOR

The Bible is filled with advice for those under temptation. While awaiting his crucifixion, Jesus told his disciples, "Watch and pray so that you will not fall into temptation. The spirit is willing, but the flesh is weak" (Matthew 26:41). Watching and praying is a strategy for life. It means thinking clearly and spiritually. Here are two more passages to help you learn how to do that.

How Jesus Fought Temptation. Read the gospel story of Jesus in the wilderness, tempted by Satan (Matthew 4:1–11). Notice the pattern of the devil's choices. The first temptation is toward physical appetite (v. 3). The second is toward pride (vv. 5–6). The third is all about power (v. 8). Why do you think Satan used this particular order, and these particular choices? How did Jesus answer each temptation?

How Believers Dress for Battle. Read Ephesians 6:10–17. Paul encourages believers to be aggressive in fighting evil. List the forms of spiritual armor and weaponry in these verses. What does each symbolize? How can you use each one to best advantage?

ETERNAL REWARDS

Temptation is a weapon of the enemy, but testing is an essential—and ultimately wonderful—act of God. The pain is only for a little while, but the rewards of faithful perseverance are eternal. Every good thing in our lives has come at a price. Your education required countless hours of study, of sitting in dull classrooms, of staying up late to prepare for tests. If you're married, it took work to make the marriage happen, then far more work to keep it going. If you're in the business world, you've paid the price of time and sacrifice for the proficiency you have.

Spiritual progress requires sacrifice, too. But it doesn't mean we have to bear it as miserable martyrs with gloomy faces. If Joseph could blossom as a slave and as a prisoner unjustly accused, can't you and I do the same in whatever dungeons we find ourselves?

Remember, the real battle is one for your spirit. The true conflict is a matter of spiritual warfare. That's how we can overcome difficult jobs and suffering marriages and challenges in health. We are citizens of heaven. That's why Paul reminds us:

Slaves, obey your earthly masters with respect and fear, and with sincerity of heart, just as you would obey Christ. Obey them not only to win their favor when their eye is on you, but as slaves of Christ, doing the will of God from your heart. Serve wholeheartedly, as if you were serving the Lord, not people, because you know that the Lord will reward each one for whatever good they do, whether they are slave or free.

—Ephesians 6:5–8

Joseph never lost the plot. He knew that the ups and downs of his life were parts of a greater story God was telling him. He never lost his grip on the dreams of what would happen one day. It might take a little blood, sweat, and tears to get there, but all of it was going to end well. Therefore, why not make this moment the best it can be? God honored that attitude. He will honor it in us, too. May you overcome temptation, and grow wise and strong in times of testing.

QUESTIONS FOR YOU

1. In your opinion, why are people drawn "close to the edge" of danger?

2. Reread the factors that made it harder for Joseph to resist temptation. What would be the factors for your life?

3. How can we be certain now that we'll be capable of thinking clearly and biblically in times of temptation?

4. What is involved in "asking Jesus Christ to handle it"? Why would this work?

5. What do you feel is the secret to maintaining a peaceful spirit when your life is being tested?

7: HEARTSICK

Coping with Deep Discouragement

CAN YOU IMAGINE stepping off a ship and walking into a vast country where you didn't know the language—and your assignment was to take the gospel to the entire nation? Add in the fact that you would be the *only* person for thousands of miles who had ever heard of Jesus Christ.

You wouldn't understand a word. Clothing, food, and customs would all be completely new to you. And the rest of your life would be spent there. That was the life chosen by missionaries during the early 1800s.

It's a little hard to believe, but until then, there were virtually no overseas missions. The whole idea of sharing the gospel in Asia or Africa or South America—it simply didn't occur to most Christians.

The first American missionary didn't begin his work until 1812. That's when Adoniram Judson arrived in Burma (now Myanmar, in Southeast Asia). Buddhism isn't a god-based religion, so the very idea of a Creator God was new to the people.

The first time he approached a local citizen, Judson's face was so filled with joy that the man later told his family he had met an angel. After that, the Burmese called Judson "Glory Face."

Judson had once been an atheist himself, committed to nothing but a life of worldly pleasure. After his conversion, he was a transformed man—one of those rare individuals ready to devote the rest

HE WROTE, "God is to me the great unknown. I believe in him, but I find him not."

of his life to sharing Christ in a culture completely new to him, as well as to any other Westerner.

But Judson couldn't have been prepared for the discouragement he would ultimately face. For one thing, he had originally wanted to go to Calcutta, but politics kept it from happening. He ultimately realized his destiny lay in Rangoon, in Burma—a place he was much more dubious about. After that, it took him seven long years to win his first convert.

Finally, just as he began to make headway, he was thrown in prison simply because the Burmese were at war with the British, and Judson (an American) was wrongly accused of being a spy. He endured seventeen months of terrible treatment in a cell overrun by vermin. Each night he was hung upside down, with only his head and shoulders on the floor. He was near to death on several occasions. He wondered where God was.

His wife would visit him, bringing their newborn child. And finally, after he was released in poor health, both his wife and child became ill and died. Judson nearly lost his mind during his period of grief. He wrote, "God is to me the great unknown. I believe in him, but I find him not."

He must have spent many hours asking some of the questions we've put forth in this book. Where was God during all his sufferings? Why should he have been thrown into prison for no crime whatsoever, other than to love the very people who imprisoned him? What would come from the life and work he had devoted to Burma, with so little result to show for so much labor? There were still few Christians in the country when Judson died after nearly forty years of missionary work there.

Now, bereaved, he entered the darkest period of his life. He sold all that he had. He returned an honorary doctorate to Brown University, and he dug a grave for himself at the edge of the jungle. Each day he came to sit beside it and think. He was very close to giving up when something light, still shining deep within his soul, led him back to God. He returned to his great work of translating the Bible into the language of Burma.[9]

Hang on to that thought. We're going to visit Adoniram Judson again near the end of this chapter. But he raises powerful questions, and these are not the first time we've faced them. Why would God treat his most beloved servants in such a way? Is there really a meaning to suffering, when it is done in the name of God?

What Judson felt, Joseph the Egyptian slave surely felt. For he, too, was accused of a crime he did not commit. He, too, was thrown into prison and left to ponder the nature of a God who seemed absent. Judson's feet were kept in shackles. Psalm 105:18 tells us that Joseph got the same treatment, and his neck was put in irons.

I would imagine both men had plenty of time simply to think about the meaning of life, and to wonder about whether their faith really made sense in a harsh and uncompromising world.

THE TEST OF TIME

During the last two chapters we considered the problem of temptation. Wayne Smith, who preached for half a century in Lexington, Kentucky, has an interesting take on that subject. He insists that the most dangerous temptation of all is not sex or money or power or any of the "brand name" temptations. He believes the most dangerous one of all is *discouragement*—the temptation to let faith dry up and wither away in the heat of life.

> **DISCOURAGEMENT is the human spirit taken ill, losing its vitality.**

Discouragement is the human spirit taken ill, losing its vitality. These days, we often give it a more serious name: *depression*. We can briefly feel discouraged; we can have a disheartening day or a ragged week. Time intensifies it and makes it a more serious issue.

There are levels of discouragement that lead to what the medical community would label as clinical depression. We know that as many as one in ten suffer from significant depression at a given time, according to statistics from the Centers for Disease Control and Prevention.[10] We know that we have something close to an epidemic of teenage depression in this generation. And perhaps the most depressed segment of our population, not surprisingly, would be people who are physically incarcerated: *prisoners*. That was the latest twist in the experience of Joseph, son of Jacob.

I can imagine the devil meeting with his demons over the problem of Joseph early on. This young man, the devil has discovered, has dreams that come straight from God. The Lord wants to use this man as a powerful servant, one who will guide the destiny of an entire nation. So the devil says, "Let's head that off at the pass. His brothers are easy to work with. We'll tempt them to sell him into slavery, and he'll never be heard from again. Joseph will be so overcome with bitterness toward his brothers he won't be able to see straight. His one goal in life will be revenge."

But that fails. Joseph resists the temptation to look back. Instead, he looks straight ahead—and straight up to God. Joseph begins to serve with excellence, so that he transcends slavery and becomes the manager of a household. He is a more impressive specimen of godliness than ever.

The devil calls another meeting. He says, "OK, we have another problem, folks. The Joseph kid was stronger than we expected, and he's back in the danger zone for being useful to our enemy. So it's time to use the old reliable: *sex*. We'll work with his master's wife, she'll come on to him, and sooner or later he has to give in. After all, he's only a man; he has his needs, right?"

But that doesn't work either. Joseph lets his no be no.

"This guy is something else," snaps the devil in severe irritation. "Bitterness wasn't enough; lust wasn't enough. It's time to play our trump card. *Discouragement* is the greatest trial of all. We'll simply wear him down. Let him slide by as the days go on, rotting away in his dungeon, of no use to anyone. He'll give up on God—and God will give up on him!"

The tests just keep coming for Joseph, each one bigger and more devastating than the last. Why can't he catch a break?

Think about men like Adoniram Judson and Joseph—vigorous, passionate, energetic men. How would you bring them down? Lock them up. Place them where they can't be productive and resourceful. Force them to brood rather than serve. Discouragement can destroy the spirit.

For years I've worked with those called to ministry. Joseph's story is a great teaching tool to show ministry as a series of trials that must be overcome, one by one. Like Judson, we go into it with a "glory face." We're filled with passion and zeal to do great things for God. And then we take that first punch. What then?

Mike Tyson said, "Everybody's got a plan until they get punched in the face."

So I ask preachers: "Can you take a punch? Do you have a plan that will hold up after you take a tough one to the jaw?" Whether you're a pastor or lawyer, a used-car salesman or a housekeeper or simply a parent, you're going to get knocked down a few times. Too many marriages are being prematurely abandoned because one of the partners doesn't have a plan for taking the first hard blow.

If you intend to slide through life, doing little to nothing for God, don't worry—the devil has no real need to work on you. It's the leaders, the doers, the people who are intent on growing and serving God, who are going to be tested. If you feel you're getting more than your share of trials, congratulations. You apparently make the demons very uncomfortable! They know God wants to do something extraordinary with your life.

That means you'll cope with some discouragement. You'll need more than a glory face—you need a glory *faith*, one that won't fall to pieces under pressure. What is involved in having a faith built to last?

SUFFERING 101
FIVE PRINCIPLES FROM THE BOOK OF JOB

The Bible's most famous treatment of the problem of suffering and discouragement is found in the book of Job. Job was a good man, a faithful servant of God, who faced a series of severe tests. Much of the book is a meditation on acts of God during suffering. Over my years of studying Job, I've gleaned at least five observations:

1. Human suffering has no easy explanation; don't even try it.
2. Being good isn't a ticket to an easy life; don't expect it.
3. God doesn't cause most suffering; don't blame him.
4. Faith is less about intellectual answers than about practical solutions; don't stop moving.
5. God's blessings are worth the wait; don't give up.

THE QUESTION OF ENTITLEMENT

Today, we give up too quickly. We give up on our marriages, our jobs, our churches, our friendships. We walk away rather than using our discouragement as a process of getting to know God better, finding out what he wants, and working to correct whatever it is that we're discouraged about.

No one likes to sit in the darkness. But tough times can offer a unique opportunity to learn about ourselves, as well as to seek God more deeply. Joseph now had to sit in the cool darkness of prison. Once, his brothers had put him in a deep hole as they decided what to do with him. Now his Egyptian brothers put him in a deeper hole, and for a much longer time. Trials intensify through life. It would have been possible to expect death to come in that unhealthy, forgotten prison.

It certainly would have been a logical time to give up—to say, "OK, I tried it God's way. I got a bad break and was sold into slavery, but I kept my nose clean. And what did God do for me? He let me end up here!"

We hear the "why me" speech a lot these days, and it's worth stopping to question its validity. Why do we all seem to think God owes us a smooth ride and maximum comfort? I've spent my life in the most prosperous nation on earth, where it's a privilege simply to be born. Yet let's say I meet a guy named Fred. Fred loses his job—takes a left hook to the jaw, as we say—and he waves his hands at the heavens and laments over how God could let such a thing happen to *him*.

Now, let's notice that Fred has seen other people lose their jobs, or much worse. Never then did Fred question the ways of God; only when something happened to him personally did the philosophical questions trouble him.

It's normal to wonder about the acts of God. But I have to wonder whether the Freds of the world have thought it through very deeply, or whether they simply feel entitled to that smooth ride. We are apparently a pampered generation. Can we handle setbacks in marriage, in career, or in anything else without feeling persecuted by the universe? Can we cope with some new program at church we don't like without leaving the church? Do we walk out on the marriage because of one unfortunate argument?

What I'm asking is whether we've lost the fine art of perseverance, which is the antidote to discouragement. To find out what that looks like, study the actions of Joseph:

> *But while Joseph was there in the prison, the LORD was with him; he showed him kindness and granted him favor in the eyes of the prison warden.*

> —Genesis 39:20–21

Now compare that passage to one from earlier in the same chapter:

The LORD was with Joseph so that he prospered, and he lived in the house of his Egyptian master. When his master saw that the LORD was with him and that the LORD gave him success in everything he did, Joseph found favor in his eyes and became his attendant.

—Genesis 39:2–4

Notice the pattern? Exactly the same thing happens in prison as in slavery. First, God is with Joseph. Second, Joseph works hard and finds favor as a result. Third, he is entrusted with greater responsibilities. Just as Potiphar completely trusted Joseph with his household, the warden completely trusts Joseph with his prison. Later, of course, the pattern will continue at the highest level yet. The leader of an empire will entrust Joseph with preparing for a coming famine. His borders will have expanded from household to prison to the world.

If we were to put it all into mathematical terms, the variable is Joseph's circumstances. The constant is Joseph's walk with God—and the attitude coming from that. Circumstances fluctuate, but attitude and faith should not. Joseph doesn't feel entitled to special treatment by God.

Weaker people have attitudes that are variables, changing with their circumstances. As long as life treats them well, they're happy people. The real test of a follower of God is whether his or her attitude can be constant as the circumstances grow tougher.

Joseph has the ability to persevere. He is not a quitter.

THE QUESTION OF EMPATHY

The first compelling quality of Joseph's character is that he doesn't feel entitled. He behaves in a prison just as he would in a palace. He spends no time on self-pity.

His second compelling quality is that he has a wonderful empathy for others. As a teenager, he has seemed insensitive to his brothers' feelings. Now, by the time he has reached his low point, he has become a person capable of ministry.

There are two new prisoners, a baker and a cupbearer. Like Joseph, they're not exactly common thieves; they've been attendants to Pharaoh, one of them a cook and the other a cupbearer (meaning he tastes the wine to check for poison). Somehow they've offended their master, and now they're locked up and in Joseph's care. Joseph is asked to oversee these two VIP inmates.

> **WHEN** we feel helpless, it's empowering to bless another human being.

When we're down and dejected, the healthiest thing we can do is to go serve someone else. Rather than being caught up in our own sorrows, carried away by self-pity, we keep a stronger perspective by helping a fellow sufferer. It takes our mind off our own struggles, and it also reminds us that others have problems, too. And there's something else: When we feel helpless, it's empowering to bless another human being.

There's another angle: We need to suffer ourselves before we can really be adept at making a difference for someone else. Have you ever tried to counsel someone on a problem you personally hadn't experienced? How about one when you'd indeed been through that very challenge? It makes a difference, doesn't it? One of the subtle acts of God is that he is always preparing us for some future ministry. Sometimes the misery of one experience leads to the joy of helping someone in another.

Ed, a friend of mine, was a minister with three grown sons. Two were strong believers, while one was rebellious. His parents loved him and tried to work with him, but trouble was a magnet that kept pulling him in. Finally Ed's son was arrested and sent to prison for dealing drugs. Ed took it very hard—so much so that he considered resigning from the ministry.

There was another preacher we'll call Frank. Frank didn't know Ed very well, but he'd heard the story and was moved to action. He called Ed and invited him to lunch. Upon picking him up, he drove the car not to a restaurant but a women's prison.

Ed wondered what was going on. Frank turned to him and said, "Ed, you wouldn't know that I have a daughter inside this prison. I drive out here sometimes, and I simply sit in the car and pray for her. I suffer deeply when I think of my girl's life in such a place."

Then he said, "Well, last week I heard your news, and I felt moved to pray for you. At least I can say I know something about what you're feeling. If you'd like to talk about it, I'm here."

Ed began talking, and soon the words were flooding from his soul, mingled in tears. He'd had no idea how much pain was dammed up inside him. But now he had a friend who understood. And when they turned the car around and drove home, both had lighter hearts. And I think I know the prayer was moving through Frank's heart: *Thank you, Lord, for using my pain. Thank you that something this ugly can be used for something so beautiful, in your gracious hands.*

Empathy is the ability to feel what another feels. It's the root of compassion, and also of our faith, which is based on a God who knows what we feel, because He put on flesh and came to experience it for himself. The Gospels tell us that Jesus looked out upon the hurting people in crowds and felt compassion for them. He loves us and gave himself for us, and our task as Christians is to "be Jesus" to others, as he has done for us. Empathy is what Hebrews 13:3 means when it tells its readers to "remember the prisoners as if chained with them" (NKJV). And not only is empathy a salve for others, it's mighty good self-medicine when we're down in the dumps.

The next time you're discouraged, do something for yourself: Help someone else. And realize that one of the reasons you're walking through this dark valley is that someone else is going to come behind you, and they'll need a fellow struggler to help show them the way.

THE ART OF PERSEVERANCE

Meanwhile, as we work through these trials, God is doing something powerful within us. Sometimes the deep wound you feel is actually the knife of the Great Physician, working to make you healthier. The greatest irony of all is that the very time when God seems the most absent is the precise time he is the most active within us. It's just that we make the mistake of confusing comfort with spiritual health.

Why do we do that? In churches, we talk about "mountaintop experiences." Those are the feel-good times, often at Christian camps or retreats, when we're off with a lot of other Christians having a great time. We feel the spiritual high, we get close to God and to each other, and it's a wonderful time. Inevitably we speak of "going back down into the valley" (the everyday world with its problems), and how sad that makes us.

The truth is that mountaintops are beautiful. Their views are unsurpassed. But fruit is not grown atop mountains, but down in the valley, the valley so low; the valley where real life happens.

Let's switch the terms from spiritual to physical for a moment. Imagine you're lying in bed at the end of the day, reading a nice book or perhaps watching a TV show. You're very comfortable and happy; life is good. The next day you go to the gym for a workout, and you couldn't feel any less comfortable. Your face wears a grimace and is coated in sweat. You're counting the moments until the session is over. But which of these two settings does the most for your health?

The answer is obvious, but let's add this observation: You need the workout *plus* perseverance. You have to push yourself over and over to get a positive effect. Walking to the car or taking an occasional flight of steps helps a little, but to get the deep training that really makes the difference, you need to be disciplined over time.

Bob Reccord of the Council for National Policy makes this point beautifully. He describes a season in his life when he knew he'd gotten out of shape physically. He wasn't pleased at all with the condition of his waistline. So he went to the gym and focused on cardiovascular exercise and weight training. He couldn't wait to see the results—if they would ever come. The workouts were tedious. All he felt afterward was *exhausted.*

Who am I kidding? he asked himself. Being stubborn, however, he wouldn't give in. He'd go to the gym if it killed him. Just as he was on the edge of judging the whole enterprise as futile, his body suddenly got into gear. The weight started melting off all at once. Muscles started to tone, and he could stay on the bicycle or the treadmill twice as long. He had gotten past the well-known "plateau," and he felt absolutely great.

"What was that all about?" he asked his doctors. They explained it to him this way: The sheer *constancy* of his training system did the trick. No matter how defeated he had felt, things were happening anyway. His body was quietly responding in ways that were beyond his senses.

"A whole new freeway system of small blood vessels and capillaries was forming within my body," he writes. "Then came the day when they decided it was time for a 'grand opening.'" More blood came rushing into the muscle tissue, like shoppers into a new superstore. And Bob was "open for business," a new and improved version of himself.

When we persevere in the midst of hard times, he concludes, the spiritual equivalent of that is occurring. It seems as if God isn't paying attention, and that life is stuck in neutral. But as we keep praying and keep trusting, the sheer constancy of faith allows God to do something down deep within us, to tone us, to bring us to a new level of spiritual fitness. And the day comes when suddenly we realize it's true— we know God with a new brand of intimacy, and when other hurting people cross our path, we'll know how to be there for them.[11]

The apostle Paul, in his letters, often has a "flowchart" approach for explaining the principles of spirituality: A leads to B, and B leads to C. I love thinking through spiritual process as he dictates it. Here is his flowchart involving perseverance:

Not only so, but we also glory in our sufferings, because we know that suffering produces perseverance; perseverance, character; and character, hope.

—Romans 5:3–4

It may seem odd to speak of "glorying in your sufferings," but can't you "glory" in a good, tough workout? Don't you get a little of the old "glory face" when your cheeks are red and you're drenched in perspiration? Why wouldn't the same principles hold true in the spirit world?

Next time you're struggling, pardon the dust. Realize that God is building a new, wiser, more mature you, and that your patient endurance is the one thing you can offer that most allows him to get that renovation done. Paul has the timetable for you:

As you suffer, you learn to persevere, because you find new strength and staying power.

As you persevere, character emerges, because you have a deeper perspective of life.

As you build character, you know what it is to hope, because you finally understand that suffering is never pointless; that God is never off duty. Instead, he is relentlessly using everything in your life to take you somewhere incredible.

THE BENEFIT OF PERSPECTIVE

It also helps to think clearly, as we know Joseph always did. In any event that occurs in your life, you can think in terms of three levels of meaning:

- What this event means for *me right now.*
- What this event means for *God's purpose for my life.*
- What this event means for *God's kingdom plan.*

Many people never get beyond that first level. They live completely in the here and now, and when life puts them in a dungeon, they can only think, "It's dark in here. Where is my next meal? When can I get out?"

The wise believer, after considering what this development means for him right now, will ask, "Yes, but what is God doing in my life? How will this contribute to his purpose for me?" And simply thinking along those lines will change things. You'll find yourself realizing, *Certainly God would want me to learn the right kind of attitude for this event. He would want me to be patient, prayerful, and hopeful. He would also want me to use this opportunity to serve someone.*

Knowing that God is at work changes the perspective. But there is one final level, and it demands the most maturity because it insists there are things more important than ourselves—than how we feel right now, or even what is happening to us over a longer period. When we consider what God might be doing for his kingdom, and how our lives are just small parts of that, we defeat the self-absorbed philosophies that dominate this world. As Rick Warren says in that famous first line of *The Purpose-Driven Life,* "It's not about me!"

If selfishness is the ultimate force behind sin—placing ourselves before God—then humility is the key to becoming the people God really wants us to be. Joseph, rather than despising those who enslaved him and then imprisoned him, loved and served those around him. As a seventeen-year-old, he was the very model of immature self-centeredness. In the big picture, his dreams were really about service, about being in a position to bless others through his leadership. But as he described them, they sounded like vanity. Later, as an Egyptian, we see only the humility in Joseph. He has become that servant; he is a man of perspective.

At the beginning of this chapter, we discussed Adoniram Judson, who lost nearly all he had while serving God. He, too, was imprisoned and, as a matter of fact, treated far more cruelly than Joseph was, if for a shorter stint. It took him years to recover, but he did find his perspective. He had to believe that, though he could see so little fruit for his labors in Burma, God had a bigger plan that someday, in eternity, he would see and understand.

Not so long ago, an anniversary was observed: the 150th anniversary of the translation of the Bible into the Burmese language. Everyone knew, of course, that this work was Judson's pride and joy. Missions professor Paul Borthwick was invited to talk about Judson to a group of interested listeners.

> **I THINK** about Judson in heaven, surrounded by 600,000 citizens of eternity who are his spiritual children.

Just before he rose to speak, he opened his Burmese Bible and saw the words, "Translated by Rev. A. Judson." Borthwick turned to his interpreter, a native of the country, and asked him what he knew about Adoniram Judson. The man began to weep. He said, "We know him. We know how he loved the Burmese people, how he suffered for the gospel because of us. He died a pauper, but left the Bible for us. When he died, there were few believers. Today there are over 600,000 of us. Every single one of us traces our spiritual heritage to one man: Rev. Adoniram Judson."[12]

I think about Judson in heaven, surrounded by 600,000 citizens of eternity who are his spiritual children. Yes, he suffered on earth, and in our limited perspective it seems unfair. At one point he could no longer see the workings of his Lord in his life, and he nearly lost his mind. But he found his way back, and I believe perspective made the difference.

He remembered the goodness of God across his life, and his faith in God's purposes was ultimately deeper than his suffering on his own account. When he died, he was joyfully awaiting a heavenly reunion, and he told his wife (he had remarried) that, while there may have been some events he didn't enjoy remembering, he had no regrets over a life given utterly to his God. And now, at the feet of Christ, Judson knows that every tear was well-spent.

Earlier I mentioned that I ask preachers whether they can take a punch. Nobody enjoys that, much less taking a *series* of them. And what about being knocked down entirely? What about being side-lined and hospitalized with a concussion and a fractured jaw? Can you praise God then? Can you get up one more time and come out swinging? Life's victors are those who have "one more get-up" in them.

Perspective makes the difference; it reminds you that God uses everything, not only for your good but for the good of his kingdom.

THE POWER OF ENCOURAGEMENT

If I were to choose any chapter of this book that I'd expect to apply to the most readers' experiences, this would be the one. After all, we're all in one of three conditions: discouraged, just over being discouraged, or just about to be discouraged. At the same time, we all have a great many acquaintances who are going through particularly tough times. Joseph's story may be more dramatic than most—we don't all get thrown into prison on trumped-up charges—but we all know what it's like to hit the bottom. There are as many kinds of prisons as there are human experiences.

So let's talk about you. What kind of cell have you found yourself in lately? Have you been treated unfairly as Joseph was? Are you wearing shackles of some kind, whether you're out of a job, struggling in marriage or with your children, or in the dumps over health issues? Maybe you can't even put your finger on it. One of the symptoms of clinical depression is an ongoing feeling of sadness without any one particular cause. Life simply isn't right; it lacks hope and excitement. You're not eager to get up in the morning.

I would invite you to ponder the three questions I've outlined in the section above:

- What do these circumstances mean for my life right now?
- What might they mean for God's purpose for my life?

- What might they mean for God's kingdom plan?

Yes, the questions get more difficult as they go on. You could spend the whole day giving chapter and verse on that first one. The second one will take some thought and some speculation, though prayer will help you with that. Ask God to show you where you can really focus your attempts at growth, just as you would focus on certain exercises in a gym. Ask him to help you remember that he's doing a great thing in your life, and *dare to be thankful* for where you are.

What's that? Be thankful for a lost job? For marital troubles? Is that crazy?

I'm not suggesting such setbacks are good in themselves, but that you can be thankful that God already has a plan to bring blessing to you through them. Once you've practiced radical, outrageous gratitude, see how that changes your mood.

For the third question, you'll receive no easy answers. Seldom does God give us a vision of the world thirty years from now or three hundred years from now, when the "little" things of today become huge realities in his plan. It's enough to ask God to remind you every day that he's a *forever* God, and not just concerned with the here and now. We need to remember that every tear is an investment. And the tears are only for a little while.

We'll pass through these trials. Joseph and Judson were released from prison. Both found their way to fulfillment and joy. That will happen for you too.

We also know that Jesus is a Savior who descends into prisons and releases captives. He went into the darkness of death on our account, and he defeated it forever. We will all see the day when the last tear has been shed, the last dungeon closed, and the last despairing question answered. We will be in his presence, then, and we'll have no more questions—only songs of praise and eternal joy.

QUESTIONS FOR YOU

1. When did you suffer most in life? What were the factors that made it so difficult?

2. What realities make discouragement, in Wayne Smith's estimation, the most dangerous temptation of all?

3. What is empathy? What is its place during times of discouragement?

4. What is Paul's "flowchart" for how God uses discouragement? How does each part lead to the following one?

5. What are three key perspective questions we should ask when encountering difficulties? How would you answer them for your current challenges?

8: BEARING THE WAIT

Surviving the Long Walk
through a Dark Valley

"WHO AM I? WHY AM I HERE?"

Those unforgettable words opened a vice-presidential debate in 1992. Everyone recognized the other two candidates: Al Gore and Dan Quayle. Admiral James Stockdale, the person speaking, knew he was "Brand X" to most voters, and he had a wry way of pointing it out.

In reality, the admiral was an American hero—one of the most highly decorated officers in the history of the United States Navy.

Jim Collins, while writing his book *Good to Great,* interviewed James Bond Stockdale—yes, his first two names were James Bond and he had lived up to it. Collins wanted to focus on the admiral's eight harrowing years as prisoner of war in Vietnam.

During a mission, Stockdale ejected from a Skyhawk plane and parachuted into a small village, where he was severely beaten and taken prisoner. Then he was placed in a tiny cell and kept in leg shackles each night, and systematically tortured on twenty more occasions during his confinement.

He quickly became the leader of prisoner resistance against the enemy captors. Stockdale organized a code of conduct that would help his fellow inmates resist the pressure to give out classified information or help the Vietnamese in any way. When he heard he would be filmed for propaganda purposes, he bruised his own face to undermine any claim the prisoners were well-treated.

Stockdale wouldn't allow any of the other prisoners of war to give up and help the Communists. And somehow he survived a harsh existence between 1965 and 1973, never knowing whether he'd ever see his loved ones again. Upon his release, he became a legend in the armed forces.

What was his secret for getting through those eight years? "I never lost faith in the end of the story," he said. "I never doubted not only that I would get out, but also that I would prevail in the end, and turn the experience into the defining event of my life, which, in retrospect, I would not trade."

A positive attitude isn't surprising. But here's the part that caught my attention. Collins asked Stockdale, "Who *didn't* make it out?"

The admiral replied, "Oh, that's easy. The optimists."

That wasn't the answer the author expected to hear, so he asked for clarification.

"The optimists," repeated Stockdale. "They're the ones who said, 'We're going to be out by Christmas.' And Christmas would come and Christmas would go. Then they'd say, 'We're going to be out by Easter.' And Easter would come and Easter would go. And then Thanksgiving, and then it would be Christmas again. And they died of a broken heart."

Admiral Stockdale then added, "This is a very important lesson. You must never confuse faith that you will prevail in the end—which you can never afford to lose—with the discipline to confront the most brutal facts of your current reality, whatever they might be."

Collins, a naturally positive communicator, says, "To this day I carry a mental image of Stockdale admonishing optimists: 'We're not getting out by Christmas; deal with it.'"

The Living Bible paraphrases 2 Corinthians 4:8–9 this way:

> *We are pressed on every side by troubles, but not crushed and broken. We are perplexed because we don't know why things*

happen as they do, but we don't give up and quit. We are hunted down, but God never abandons us. We get knocked down, but we get up again and keep going.

That's the attitude of a can-do survivor who refuses to give in. Not surprisingly, it was written by a prisoner: Paul. It exemplifies two other prisoners: Joseph and James Stockdale. But what exactly is the difference between that attitude and everyday, run-of-the-mill optimism?

We've wrapped our minds around the fact that two things can coexist: a good God and a bad time. Trusting God offers no guarantees that everything will proceed as we would script it. In earlier chapters, we discussed some of the reasons that we must

> **WHAT DO** we do when we continue to be disappointed as the months pile up?

endure sorrow, tragedy, and deep disappointment in this life. The most basic level, we've agreed, is learning to live with setbacks.

But there's another level of growth, and it's much more demanding. Not every believer is successful at this level. We come to a point when we must accept discouragement compounded by the passing of time. We must bear the wait, life's heaviest burden.

What do we do when we continue to be disappointed as the months pile up? We should keep a positive spirit and pray, of course—we realize that. We can't lose faith in the "end of the story." Even so, we're free to pray from the heart and tell God what we really want, even when we don't seem to be getting it. No one who is hanging from a cliff, holding on with one hand, is going to pray, "If it's your will, Father—don't let me fall. If not, well, that's fine, too."

No, unless you're crazy, your prayer will be more concise: "Help!"

It's all right to tell God the desires of your heart. But what happens when he says no?

God didn't answer my prayer. Oh, he answered it—just not as you might have hoped. It has been said he has four answers: *Yes, No, Maybe,* and *You've got to be crazy!*

If you think about it, our problem isn't that we don't get our prayers answered, but that we don't get them answered in our way and on our timetable.

These are defining moments for your faith. You come to a fork in the road, and you must choose a path:

- The path of walking away from faith, because it no longer seems real.
- The path that leads deeper into the knowledge and wisdom of God, disappointments and all.

The first path is for travelers who believe faith equals getting what we want. Once that "agreement" seems to have been violated by God, the relationship is declared null and void.

The second path clings to God all the more in disappointment, believing that it is these very moments when we experience him in the deepest way. It is about trusting God because he is real and because that's what life is about—whether we get what we immediately want or not. This path never "dies of a broken heart," because the events themselves only strengthen the heart.

I find it very compelling that Admiral Stockdale was carried forward by a certain kind of optimism while dismissing a *different* variety of it. It's a powerful insight, isn't it? Cheap, superficial optimism isn't only worthless—it's bad for our health. The optimists finally gave up in Stockdale's prison; yet he believed he "would prevail in the end, and turn the experience into the defining event of [his] life."

Superficial optimists are hurt deeply by the fact they can't "positive-think" their way to happiness. Once their worldview falls apart, life no longer seems to make sense. Reality-grounded optimists, on the other hand, see God working in *all* events, and actually claim to learn the most about God in the difficult times.

What we learn is that God wastes nothing. Unless we let our discouragement become a cancerous spirit, the Lord will use it for something precious and priceless—a deep wisdom that will serve us and those around us for the rest of our lives.

DREAMS IN THE DARKNESS

When we last saw Joseph, at the end of Genesis 39, his roller-coaster life had reached the top and taken the vicious downward turn again. He was falsely accused of rape, then thrown into the royal prison, where he may never have been heard from again.

That didn't happen, of course. We've already noticed two patterns in Joseph's circumstances. Just as he'd gotten to work making life simpler for Potiphar, his old master, now he did the same for the prison warden. "So the warden put Joseph in charge of all those held in the prison, and he was made responsible for all that was done there" (Genesis 39:22).

In the last chapter we observed that one of the secrets of handling tough times is to get up and get busy. When you're unsure about the acts of God—get your own act together.

Admiral Stockdale did that, and so did Joseph. The irony is that Joseph had been known to his family as "the dreamer." Dreamers of a certain type aren't survivors, according to Stockdale. Escapist dreamers fail to found their hopes in the urgent reality before them. Joseph wasn't like that. He was now a doer rather than a dreamer. On the other hand, he still had the special gift that God had given him—the ability to discern what God was saying through dreams and visions.

Does God still speak in dreams? Throughout the Old Testament, and even on a few occasions in the New, God delivers vital messages through this medium. God speaks in many ways, but we need to be careful on this point today. For one thing, the Holy Spirit has come;

he was not available before Christ. Since the day of Pentecost, just after the resurrection, we've had the presence of the Spirit inside every believer to help us discern the voice of God, speaking into our lives. We also have the full Old and New Testaments—the Word of God—that very clearly tell us his will on various subjects.

Yet there are occasions when God speaks in a dramatic way, and these occasions may have been much more common in the ancient world, before Jesus.

Among the prisoners in Joseph's care were two from the Pharaoh's kitchen. The baker and the cupbearer had offended their ruler in some way, and now they were in prison. On the same night, each of them had a dream.

We know that some time had gone by, because Joseph was already present when they checked in. The dreams came "some time later" (see Genesis 40:4). So keep in mind that Joseph was already seeing his life flow by in the dust and decay of a prison. If God was doing something, it wasn't apparent. On the other hand, it had to be strange that both these men came to him with enigmatic dreams on the same day. A person of faith is spiritually vigilant, watching for an opportunity to serve God. That's what happened here.

Joseph asked the two men why they were so dejected, and they told him they had no one to interpret their dreams. Joseph replied, "Do not interpretations belong to God? Tell me your dreams" (v. 8). Joseph gave God the glory for his gift even before using it. This is a clue to the state of his faith at that point.

Both men had dreams that made use of imagery from their occupations. The cupbearer had a dream involving a grapevine. Joseph listened to the details and told him its meaning: Within three days, Pharaoh was going to grant the cupbearer a pardon.

Joseph added a personal note: "But when all goes well with you, remember me and show me kindness; mention me to Pharaoh and get me out of this prison" (v. 14). He went on to offer the details of how he had come to Egypt without doing anything to deserve imprisonment.

The baker, encouraged by the interpretation he had heard, then told his dream—without the same results. Pharaoh was to have him beheaded within three days, Joseph said. It couldn't have been enjoyable being the bearer of those tidings, but Joseph himself had observed that interpretations came from God.

And sure enough, both events transpired just as Joseph had foretold.

TIME AND TRIBULATION

Now, Joseph only had to play the waiting game.

Only? We all know there's nothing more frustrating than waiting for something to take place. Men in particular can handle almost anything better than waiting. They're eager and action-based. But patience is a hard-won virtue for men and women alike.

Joseph had to feel that it couldn't be long before he would hear something to his advantage. He had given the cupbearer the best possible news. Surely the man would waste no time before telling the authorities, "Say, there's this good man you need to know about, and someone needs to review his situation . . ."

For Joseph, things were different now. Every morning must have dawned on wings of hope. If he had prayer partners, he would have been telling them, "Pray hard for me! I've been waiting all this time, and it looks like God is doing something—I had the opportunity to help a man close to the Pharaoh; surely that's no mere coincidence! God is faithful, and he is about to bring me out of this darkness."

But the cupbearer "did not remember Joseph; he forgot him" (v. 23). It's one of the more heartbreaking lines in all the Old Testament. And Joseph was left to figure this out through the silence that followed day after day after lengthy day—730 days, for the Bible tells us two years passed. We're left to imagine the new dimensions of heartbreak

Joseph had to face. Like James Stockdale, he must have asked himself, "Who am I? Why am I here?" But to his credit, he never placed his hope in fantasies; he simply kept trusting God.

Waiting. It's actually one of the Bible's great themes.

Abraham and Sarah had to wait twenty-five years to see God fulfill the most outrageous of promises, that they would bear a child even when they were old.

Moses had to wait forty years in the wilderness before God showed him his great mission in life.

David had to run for his life, living in forests and caves, after being ordained as the next king. He waited more than a decade before his coronation.

Paul's first missionary journey didn't occur until ten years after his Damascus Road conversion experience.

By comparison, Joseph's wait in prison was only two years after the cupbearer left—but they were *prison* years, meaning life moved in slow motion. But I'm guessing you understand that. I would bet that you know what it is to wait through tough times. The intensity of suffering is amplified by the time of its duration.

Some of us are waiting to meet someone we might like to marry. Others, like Abraham and Sarah, are waiting for the announcement that a child will come to fill their lives. Some, like Moses, are waiting to discover what God has in store as their life work. The hours and days and decades we spend waiting are among the most trying. That's why they're the most spiritually useful to God in transforming us to be the people it is our destiny to become:

Abraham, worthy to found a nation because he knew how to wait upon the Lord.

Moses, worthy to lead a nation to its home because he had waited and matured.

David, worthy to become the nation's greatest king because of his hard-won wisdom.

Paul, worthy to be the architect of early Christianity because he had waited on the Lord.

9 QUESTIONS FOR THOSE WAITING ON GOD

When God doesn't seem to be answering your prayer, here are a few questions to guide your thinking:

1. Have I been consistent and patient in praying?
2. Whom have I trusted to pray with me?
3. Will the answer I'm seeking best serve God's kingdom?
4. Could God be saying, "Not yet," and why?
5. Has God answered my prayer in a way I failed to recognize?
6. Is unconfessed sin coming between God and me?
7. What does God want to do within me as I wait?
8. Could God be waiting for me to take some action on my own?
9. Will I praise God whatever his answer may be?

WHEN GOD SAYS NO

How is faith cultivated and built up?

When the seas are calm and the weather is sunny, most of us can be strong followers of Christ. But what happens when we find ourselves waiting, because God has said no—and continues to say no?

Not long ago, I knew two men who were experiencing what may be the most difficult trial life can bring: losing a child. In both cases, these were men who knew they might lose an adult child. The fathers prayed harder than they ever had, prevailing upon God to spare their loved ones. And they were both surrounded by networks of people praying on their behalf.

Tragically, neither adult child was spared.

In one case, the father told me, "My heart is broken. This is the deepest pain I've ever encountered, and I know there's a hole in my heart that won't be healed in this life. You never get over something like this. But I have no issues with God; I've told him that I don't have to understand his ways to accept them, and he knows that I can live with the hope of seeing my child again someday in heaven. That hope is very special to me."

The other father simply couldn't accept what happened. When he saw his prayers go unanswered, he walked away from his faith and disassociated himself from his church.

When discussing tragic situations like those, we must begin by saying, "There but for the grace of God go I." No one would wish to have his faith tested in such a way. But there is biblical precedence for such a test. God asked Abraham to offer his son Isaac on the altar as a sacrifice (Genesis 22). That sacrifice, of course, never occurred because God stopped it. What then was it all about?

The crucial point is that Abraham didn't *know* God would stop it—he had to walk in faith, even when he couldn't understand what God was doing. As a result, Abraham's faith was so sturdily proven that he was ready to be the father of a great nation. He had demonstrated it by showing that even the dearest thing in his life would not come before his obedience to God. Tests reveal how genuine and strong our faith is.

Let's also remember that God submitted himself to the same "test"—but he didn't withhold his own Son from sacrifice. If Abraham proved how much he loved God, God proved how much he loved you and me by offering his own Son in the sacrifice that did have to take place.

How have you responded when God said no? What was revealed

about your faith? It's a serious question for a very pampered society in which few of us are asked for any real sacrifice.

I'm an avid basketball fan, and I read an article recently about men

> **OPTIMISM** is fine; *blind* optimism, however, is a very questionable policy.

pursuing their dreams of playing professional basketball. The ages of the two men in the story were thirty-nine and forty-one. One of them paid nearly $1,700 to fly from Budapest to Louisville for a tryout in minor league basketball. He was six feet tall and forty-one years old. Maybe I'm not enough of a wild-eyed dreamer, but it seems to me that if your body is a certain age and bears certain measurements, your faith in a dream of playing basketball is not reality-based.

Optimism is fine; *blind* optimism, however, is a very question-able policy. There comes a time for accepting the conditions of the real world and realizing that God has given us what we need to do the things we need to do. We have in our world a lot of Peter Pans—boys (and girls) who "won't grow up." Dreaming isn't enough. We need to know God's dreams for us, because the truth is they will give us far more contentment than the dreams we began with.

One of the great truths about those occasions when God says no is this: God's eventual yes is better and wiser, and someday we'll be thankful that his will was done.

NAME IT, CLAIM IT

Therefore our first insight about surviving a lengthy period of discouragement is to realize that God sometimes says no. Faith is not psyching yourself into believing that God is about to come through and you simply need to pray harder; faith is aligning yourself with the will of God, which is sometimes different from our own.

During the last half-century or so, one of the most disturbing developments in church life has been the growth of what we call the "prosperity gospel" or the "gospel of health and wealth." These preachers tell people exactly what they want to hear: that God's greatest goal is for them to be comfortable. Scripture verses are twisted until they're unrecognizable in the attempt to show that if we simply want something badly enough (usually something fairly selfish) then God will give it to us. If someone gets sick and dies, it's only because people didn't pray enough, they say—everyone should be healed. If someone else is struggling financially, it's only because he didn't claim the financial prosperity God wanted him to have.

It's easy to understand why some people flock to hear such a pleasing message, but it's not what the Bible is about; it completely denies the possibility of God saying no.

But wait—aren't there passages in the Bible telling us that we can ask anything in God's name, and believing, we shall receive? Don't verses like these serve as all-purpose coupons we can redeem during prayer, so that we can have anything we'd like?

No, of course not. The whole counsel of Scripture tells a different story. Those prayer promises assume we have a closeness to God that brings us into line with what he wants. God wants us to have the adventure of coming to know him so intimately that his mind infects ours with its desires, and we want the things he wants; we love people as he loves them; his priorities become our priorities.

We can't have everything we want. The apostle Paul would bear testimony to that. In 2 Corinthians 12:7–10, Paul discusses an occasion when he had an infirmity of some kind—something he will only call a "thorn in my flesh, a messenger of Satan, to torment me" (v. 7). Three times he prayed to God for deliverance. You would think that when someone was under satanic attack, that would be a prayer that deserved a "yes" answer. But God had other ideas. He told Paul, "My grace is sufficient for you, for my power is made perfect in weakness" (v. 9).

Paul believed God allowed the infirmity because the apostle needed humbling (v. 7). Coping with it kept him in a spirit of prayer and dependence upon God. And in time, Satan's attack was co-opted to become God's ministry to Paul's spirit. He learned a tough, self-disciplined reliance on God that would serve him later, as things grew tougher in his life.

When you're wrestling with some unwelcome factor in your life, and God won't remove it, could the same thing be happening? Could it be that He simply wants a little more of your attention? So much of the time, it takes misfortune to turn our hearts back to God.

FATHER KNOWS BEST

I have a young grandson who is 100 percent little boy. For one thing, he says exactly what's on his mind. One of the great joys of my life is in listening to some of the hilarious observations that flow from his mouth.

If he wants something, nothing could stop him from asking for it. Last year he told my wife and me what he had in mind for his next birthday: the latest high-tech video game console. I quickly noted the $200 price tag it carried. Toys have come a long way since building blocks and little red wagons.

I smiled and asked my grandson why he thought we'd get him something that "special." He quickly replied, "Because you love me so much! And because I want it so much!"

I can't argue with him on either count. We'd do almost anything for our grandson. After his parents took him to Florida to live, autumn came and he said, "I miss going to Nanna's house and jumping in the leaves." So we boxed up several bags of fallen leaves and sent them via UPS, at $40 shipping, so he could jump around in them to his heart's content.

So, he can feel his grandparents' love in a number of ways. And one of them *could* be the gift of a $200 video game console. Except we said no. Why?

First, because he's just a little guy, and if he is given too many good things too fast, it will spoil him. That's not something you understand at his age; only through the wisdom of years. If he receives everything he asks for, he won't be ready for the disappointments life has in store later. At this point, it's a helpful exercise for him to learn about limits.

Second, he's not our only grandchild, just one in a series of seven. We're scrupulous about spreading our love equally because we love them equally. If we set a $200 precedent, we'll have a $1,400 per year birthday expense for our grandchildren. (Double it if you want to count Christmas!)

We'd much rather give them smaller gifts, while making better donations toward their college education. Do the younger ones understand that? Probably not. But someday they will.

We're all so much like children before a perfect Father whose wisdom is over our heads most of the time. We only know what we want, and that we want it *now*. In some cases, he knows we need the exercise of waiting for the betterment of our souls. If he gave us everything, it would ruin us.

In other cases, he must measure the fact that we are not his only children. One of his children is praying to win *American Idol*, but another child is praying the same thing. One of his children has spotted Mr. Right and is praying that God will make him love her—but another child has the same request.

We are all part of a vast picture, a mosaic assembled by God's loving hands. As tiny parts of that picture, we can only see a color or two surrounding us, while God stands back and sees it all. He knows the patterns. He knows the final image. And to create the perfect picture he has in mind—the picture still coming together—he must sometimes say no.

Someday, at the right time, my grandson will have that game console. If not, he'll have a much better one that has since been introduced to game-crazy kids. And when he does, his joy and excitement will be enhanced because that gift didn't come so easily. He paid his dues in *waiting*. He learned emotional discipline. And that's a gift far more valuable than the one he thought he was asking for.

While we're telling God what we want, he is always giving us what we need.

SECRETS OF WAIT CONTROL

We've seen that waiting is a great theme in the Scriptures, but there is a particular way the Bible teaches us to do it. We are to *wait upon the Lord.* It's one of the great arts of living as a believer in this world, and it seems we have too few "artists" of this medium in our time.

Waiting upon the Lord is both attitude and action. In this chapter we've seen how Joseph and Admiral Stockdale each had the right mindset and the right skill set. The attitude is all about trusting God, knowing that he is in control and things will work out as they should, even when we can't understand all the dimensions of God's greater wisdom. This is the emotional discipline we've discussed, knowing that we're making an investment in tears that reaps dividends in our soul.

The active part is continuing in obedience to God, serving others, working for his kingdom, and preparing ourselves to be the best workers we can be when he is ready to bless us. James advises us:

> *Be patient, then, brothers and sisters, until the Lord's coming. See how the farmer waits for the land to yield its valuable crop, patiently waiting for the autumn and spring rains. You too, be patient and stand firm, because the Lord's coming is near.*
>
> —James 5:7–8

Why does the farmer wait? Because he knows the secrets of growth. He understands that he can't plant a seed today and eat a carrot tomorrow. He'll have to wait for the proper cycle.

On the other hand, after he waits, he won't receive just one carrot; each one will produce seeds for what can ultimately be an *infinite* number of carrots. We ask for simple, passing things—video consoles instead of spiritual wisdom; candy instead of the bread of life. But God does "immeasurably more than all we ask or imagine, according to his power that is at work within us" (Ephesians 3:20). Our requests, in the great scheme of things, are small enough; God's gifts are infinite and eternal.

If we can understand that, we can learn to wait.

Then, when it seems we have nothing else to cling to, we can remember we have this promise:

> *But those who wait on the Lord*
> *Shall renew their strength;*
> *They shall mount up with wings like eagles,*
> *They shall run and not be weary,*
> *They shall walk and not faint.*
>
> —Isaiah 40:31 nkjv

The New International Version translates the phrase in that first line as "*hope* in the Lord." In other words, waiting is a form of hoping. And there's nothing passive about it—not like sitting on the sofa checking your watch with impatience. No, this is a form of waiting drenched in solid hope and eager belief, and it doesn't sit still. Waiting on God has a special energy.

I think of a basketball team preparing for its big tournament game. In the period before tip-off, the players don't sit on the bench, waiting and staring at their shoes. They're on the court, warming up. You can see the vitality as they move around, taking layups, practicing passes, chattering to each other—all systems are go. Even when a player doesn't have a ball in his hands, he's going through the motions of a hook shot just as if he does. The adrenaline is flowing; no way could they sit still.

That's the kind of waiting Isaiah talks about—energetic, enthusiastic, active waiting. Isaiah says that people who wait like that find new strength; they soar like eagles, run without weariness, and walk without fainting. That's the way Joseph waited on the Lord. That's the way Christians throughout the ages have waited, even when they felt discouraged; even when they couldn't imagine what God was up to. Paul thanked God for his chains, because they gave him the chance to share his faith with the guards.

As the song says, when these people can't trace God's hand, they trust his heart.

When you're on a long walk through a dark valley, you need that kind of hope and strength—with a faith that isn't blind, but reality-based, because the reality is this: *God loves you.* As Stockdale put it, don't lose faith in the end of the story, because this is the greatest story ever told.

You won't walk through this valley forever. So trust God's heart. Know that he loves you, no matter what the skies look like. And walk on.

QUESTIONS FOR YOU

1. In Admiral Stockdale's story, what two kinds of "optimism" (another word for faith) are discussed? What are the differences?

2. What factors make time a formidable test in itself? For what reasons might God make us wait?

3. How does our response to God's "no" define us spiritually? How has that happened in your life?

4. In what ways is God like a father in the way he responds to our requests?

5. What are you waiting for in life right now? How can you be more intentional about "waiting on the Lord"?

9: BLESSING AND TESTING

Making the Most of Sunny Seasons

I HAVE A SOFT PLACE in my heart for a James Stewart movie.

He can be in cowboy mode, or mystery mode, or in the role of George Bailey in *It's a Wonderful Life*. If Stewart's in the movie, I find I'll probably like it.

Shenandoah, a 1965 film, is one of the good ones. Stewart plays his usual type of character: a quiet pillar of strength and integrity who can get tough when a crisis comes. In this story, the crisis is the Civil War. Stewart's character is a farmer who holds his large family all the closer because his wife has died. Some of his sons are eager to march off to war, but their father wants the world and its problems to go away.

Early in the film, Stewart gathers the family for dinner. There's an empty place at the table where his wife would have sat. In his familiar drawl, Stewart begins what seems to be his standard speech before Sunday dinner: "Now your mother wanted all of you raised as good Christians," he explains, "and I might not be able to do that thorny job as well as she could, but I can do a little something about your manners."

So every head is bowed and every eye closed as he launches into a surprisingly self-satisfied prayer: "Lord, we cleared this land, we plowed it, sowed it, and harvested it. We cooked the harvest. We wouldn't be here, we wouldn't be eatin', if we hadn't done it all ourselves. We worked dog-boned hard for every crumb and morsel, but we thank you just the same anyway, Lord, for the food we're about to eat. *Amen*."

Then, in the course of the movie, life happens. The farmer can't shield his family from a bloody war. Tragedies occur, and finally we have a scene in which Stewart's character sits down to dinner again. This time there are several more empty chairs, and the farmer doesn't sit as tall. He's no longer possessed so much by the pride of accomplishment. His voice cracks as he comes before God in a lowlier spirit, reflecting that he no longer sees himself as the captain of his own fate. And his final words are, "if we hadn't done it all ourselves."

Like so many people, the farmer had fallen prey to the illusion that whatever was in his hands, he had only himself to thank for it. He held a slightly grudging place for God in the conversation, just as he held a seat for his absent wife. But like Job in the Bible, he was driven by loss toward a spiritual reckoning of his true place in the world. Within the goodness of blessing lies a hidden curse: the tendency toward spiritual laxity.

Most of us can handle adversity better than we ever expected—it's prosperity that sabotages the spirit. Thomas Carlyle, the Scottish essayist, said, "Adversity is hard on a man, but for every one man who can stand prosperity there are one hundred who can stand adversity."

Tough times cause us to question where God went. But that's very often a good thing, because it sends us looking for him. In our pain and our grief, we come after him when there is nowhere else to turn. Then, when the sun comes out again and life is good—God wonders where *we* went.

THE PROBLEM WITH COMFORT

This is really one of the great recurring themes in all of the Bible: people who walked with God into the sunshine, then simply wandered away because they forgot who made the sun. Israel's first king, Saul, was so humbled by his coronation that he hid from the masses. But it only took a little time on the throne, a little honor, a little easy life to turn him arrogant and faithless. By the time he began hunting down his successor, David, he was no longer the same man but a twisted, embittered version of himself. He couldn't handle prosperity.

David, the next in line, was called a man after God's own heart. He was gifted, handsome, and deeply spiritual—and after a few years, he was capable of serious sin. For a while, he lost the unique intimacy with God that had made him special. His long years of hiding in forests and caves had made him who he was. Great, inspired psalms came from those times. But the easy life corroded his devotion.

David's son Solomon became the third king. His first official act was to ask God for the wisdom to lead. God granted his request. But as time passed, the elder Solomon ignored his best wisdom. He became a deeply flawed man who allowed false gods in the palace.

But we don't have to open our Bibles for examples. It happens to us, and it happens all around us.

How often have we seen it in politics, where power corrupts? How often in the world of sports? The athletic world is filled with prodigal sons, disciplined and driven athletes who became twenty-five-year-old millionaires and squandered their God-given talents for wild living.

In so many ways, we've seen it happen in our country. The "Greatest Generation" was the product of a Great Depression and great war. These were times of sacrifice, prayer, and national unity, and they built the United States into the leader of the free world. But the prosperity that resulted became a corrupting influence. We became a wealthy people, and morals began to erode. People began to turn from God, thinking, as James Stewart's farmer thought, that they "did it all themselves."

> **IT TAKES** a true and serious follower of Christ to handle prosperity.

Prosperity comes to us and says, "Kick back. Relax. Grab for some gusto. You've worked hard, and now you can enjoy yourself. Eat, drink, and be merry." What we don't realize is that the human soul is like a garden. It must be tended. It needs care and nurture, or the roses wither, and the weeds rise up to choke them out.

So it takes a seeker of God to handle adversity well, but it takes a true and serious follower of Christ to handle prosperity. J. Oswald Sanders wrote, "Not everyone can carry a full cup."

We've followed the tests of Joseph throughout this book. As a young man, he didn't handle easy times particularly well, but we can forgive most of that as the folly of youth. What we recognize is that a rugged fate was the making of his character. And with each test, we see him emerge as a more impressive man of God.

First, of course, he must undergo the temptation to give up on God when he faces the harsh realities of being sold into slavery. He refuses to do that, and he passes this test.

Second, he undergoes sexual temptation, and comes through with his integrity intact.

Third is the temptation toward bitterness when he is unjustly accused—he does the time without having done the crime. But again, he transforms his environment through godly behavior.

Fourth is the temptation to simple despair. He helps a fellow prisoner who is pardoned, but who then forgets to return the favor by putting in a good word for Joseph. Still, Joseph has a light that shines on in the darkness of his prison. Doubt may have been whispering in his ear: *You've remembered God; why doesn't he remember you?*

All of these temptations had one thing in common: adversity. And none of them worked. So what's ahead for Joseph and his spiritual obstacle course?

We must once again imagine the devil, gathering his demons in the conference room for the Monday meeting. He launches into an angry monologue about the ineptness of his Joseph committee. He's really breathing fire today—hellfire and brimstone even by his standards.

"Persecution!" he shouts, pointing at the demon who specializes in it. "All you did was make things worse. Lust! What a failure you were! Bitterness! Despair! You call *that* tempting? You losers couldn't tempt a fish into water."

These demons all hang their heads. Satan's not exactly "boss of the year" material, but they've never seen him this worked up.

Then, from the back of the room comes the sound of a throat being cleared. "Excuse me," says a newcomer. "My name is Blessing."

The devil says, "You've got the wrong meeting. And I mean *wrong*. I hope you've filled your tank, because you've got a long drive . . ."

"Excuse me, but I'm very much in the right place," says the newcomer. "Just hear me out." He then stands and shares his idea.

Satan scratches his goatee and thinks for a moment. "You know what? It's just crazy enough that it might work."

PHARAOH'S DOUBLE DREAM

When two full years had passed, Pharaoh had a dream.
—Genesis 41:1

Dreams again! Joseph must be wondering if they're ever going to actually *help* him. But he realizes that God is the instigator of all the great turning points in this story. From the beginning, God has had a plan for Joseph, a plan for Joseph's nation, and a plan for Egypt. Through dreams, God has hinted at matters of national destiny.

As a young man, Joseph was the one with the dreams—and he used them for boasting. Now, if Joseph himself still receives these visions from heaven, we're not told. A humbler man, he is a mere interpreter of others' dreams. And Joseph knows that still, he is only the mouthpiece. He says, "Do not interpretations belong to God?" (Genesis 40:8).

This time it is no less than Pharaoh himself who has a double feature of very bizarre dreams. He wakes up and knows that something significant, something greater than himself, is happening. He has seen seven fat cows gobbled up by seven skinny ones in the first dream. The second is similar, but it involves heads of grain. It would be nice to think he'd just eaten too much rich food late at night, but the repeated pattern makes it clear—a message is trying to get through.

Determined to break the code, Pharaoh convenes all his magicians and wise men. But they have no magic or wisdom to offer. This was a culture that acknowledged 2,000 different gods and goddesses. They collected them out of the air the way we collect TV channels from the satellite dish. And as we all know, the more channels we have, the harder it is to find anything worth watching. That's how it is on this day for Pharaoh—2,000 deities and none of them coming through.

It's this moment when the cupbearer, Joseph's old friend, suddenly turns very pale at the mention of dreams. He steps forward humbly and says, "Today I am reminded of my shortcomings" (v. 9).

Indeed! He is there because of a good friend who could interpret dreams, and that good friend is still locked up because the cupbearer has failed him. Now, to his credit, he admits his sin of omission; he tells Pharaoh about Joseph. The prisoner is finally summoned, cleaned, given a fresh shave and presentable clothes, and given a pair of dreams to sort out.

Joseph is probably thinking, "This is really happening. *Finally.*" He has been in that prison for a long time now—two years since the cupbearer left. For us, time seems to move at its own strange speed. It can bolt like a stallion or be still and unmoving as a great rock. But "with the Lord a day is like a thousand years, and a thousand years are like a day" (2 Peter 3:8). God created time and is not subject to it. He uses it as he uses all things in creation, for his own purposes. We can be sure that Joseph was in that prison precisely as long as God wanted him to be there, to the second—because God was doing a wonderful thing in the life of Joseph.

A lesser man would step into the presence of this elite ruler, gaze around the lofty throne room, and think, *I'd better be a smooth operator.*

Then he might say, "If I interpret your dream, will you grant me amnesty?" He might also figure it couldn't hurt to provide a very flattering interpretation to Pharaoh's dream. But Joseph is trusting completely in God, and he knows that interpretations belong to the Lord. "I cannot do it," he says, "but God will give Pharaoh the answer he desires" (v. 16).

So Joseph hears about the plump cows and the scrawny ones, the fat grain and the withered, and the answer must seem so obvious to him that he wonders why everyone in the room can't already see it. But that's just the way it is when you're walking in the Spirit; you see issues with a clarity others don't possess.

As everyone sits spellbound, Joseph explains that seven years of prosperity are coming, followed by seven years of famine. And to be forewarned is to be fore-armed.

We might have expected a few court magicians to scoff. After all, they've just been shown up by a convict, and a foreign slave convict at that. But the room remains silent as Joseph calmly dictates what should happen next, in full, intelligent detail. He offers no less than a national policy for ascending to even greater power through a world famine.

Joseph, of course, knows a little bit about good times and hard times.

PURPOSE AND PLAN

I believe the people in Pharaoh's presence knew wisdom when they heard it. Eternity is planted in our hearts, as the Scriptures tell us, and people instinctively recognize God's truth when they hear it. Also, we know when we're in the presence of a true leader, someone who knows the way. Joseph was such a man. His strength, like a sword, had been forged in fire, and no one dared to dispute him.

Joseph's advice here is a bit like wise retirement planning: Take a portion of the overflow during good times, and it will tide you over during the winter of your life. To stand before a king and give such counsel took some *chutzpah*. But Joseph had been a man who impressed others in every kind of environment. When God's hand is on your life, it doesn't really matter whether you stand in a damp prison or an extravagant palace—you'll make an impression. Eventually Pharaoh turns to his advisors and says, "Can we find anyone like this man, one in whom is the spirit of God?" (v. 38).

It must have been one of those moments when everyone was humbled by the visible workings of God. For Joseph, it was all his trust, all his obedience through the years coming to fruition. For Pharaoh, it was the realization that among 2,000 useless gods and goddesses, there was one genuine deity, and one reliable spokesman for him. For the others there, perhaps it was simply a time to keep silent in the company of greatness.

Joseph pointed out that because this dream came in a matching set of two—cattle and grain—it meant "the matter has been firmly decided by God, and God will do it soon" (v. 32). For now, of course, Pharaoh made the bold move of appointing this man—a mangy prisoner a few moments ago—to a position of vast power, with the future of Egypt in his hands. "Only with respect to the throne will I be greater than you," said the Pharaoh (v. 40). He was "all in" with the impressive interpreter of dreams.

In some ways, it seems an unlikely move for a world leader to make. Yet we must remember that "in the LORD's hand the king's heart is a stream of water that he channels toward all who please him" (Proverbs 21:1). This verse refers to an aqueduct that channels water onto a mill wheel to grind grain. History is like a flowing river, and God can reach into the flow and change its course at any time.

In that moment, when the interpretation of the two dreams came across so clearly and powerfully, Pharaoh must have realized that a genuine and true God was guiding his nation's destiny. It made sense to show the utmost deference to that God's spokesman.

It's a wonderful moment in life when all puzzle pieces fit and form their picture, when the acts of God show the wisdom they held all along. Joseph now understands what his sufferings have brought him: patience, obedience, submission, perseverance, and heightened gifts of listening and management. When his moment arrives, he is ready for it.

Joseph had been cocky. He'd been gifted as a young man, and he'd known it. What he couldn't have known was that there was so much to do before God could really use him. And it's really by the grace of God that we're not given advance notice before we begin our studies in the school of hard knocks.

THE TEST OF THE BLESSED

Genesis 41:42–45 tells us just how radically Joseph's life changed now. He had an unlimited expense account to use for the country's service. He wore impressive clothing and a gold chain. He was issued a chariot, and with it came public recognition as he wheeled by the pyramids: "Look, there's that new guy everyone's talking about—the Hebrew slave who's going to help us head off a recession!" He had a new name, a new wife—a new life. Good things come to those who wait.

But as we've seen, these good things come disguised as the final payoff, when in reality they are the final playoff. This is the championship game of the spirit. It's one thing—and a highly commendable one—to come through adversity intact. But how are we going to handle prosperity?

This is the very reason Jesus spoke about rich men struggling to enter the kingdom of God, saying that it is harder than a camel's attempt to get through the eye of a needle. The fatter we become, the harder it is to squeeze ourselves onto that narrow path. Wealthy and comfortable people must battle the constant temptations of pride, self-indulgence, false security, laziness, greed, materialism, and all the tangible things that would distract us from the true and intangible things of God.

Later, his father Jacob's descendants spent nearly forty years without a home, wandering in the wilderness. When the time finally came for their trial to end, and for them to enter their Promised Land, God gave them a strict warning:

> *Be careful that you do not forget the LORD your God, failing to observe his commands, his laws and his decrees that I am giving you this day. Otherwise, when you eat and are satisfied, when you build fine houses and settle down . . . you may say to yourself, "My power and the strength of my hands have produced this wealth for me." But remember the LORD your God, for it is he who gives you the ability to produce wealth, and so confirms his covenant, which he swore to your ancestors, as it is today.*
> —Deuteronomy 8:11–12, 17–18

James Stewart's farmer could attest to the truth of that passage. The full cup is the hardest to carry. In good times, we feel as if we've crossed the finish line. The reporter runs up to us, thrusts a microphone in front of us, and says, "Now that you've finally won the Super Bowl, what are you going to do now?" And the world expects us to say, "I'm going to Disney World!" Or to throw a huge party. Or at least to relax and catch up on a little sleep. Isn't life a cycle of work and reward?

Yes, to an extent. But the counsel of Scripture is to keep on walking. Keep on obeying. Keep on listening to what God has to say, because now the soul will be tried more seriously than ever. We'll be tempted to say, with James Stewart's farmer, "I did this all by myself—but all the same, thank you kindly, Lord."

A certain familiar business cycle has been described as "employ, enjoy, destroy." It describes organizations that rise through hard work and long hours—only to become victims of their own success. Once the profit level soars, the executives mentally check out. They lose their edge—their focus has taken off for Disney World.

So we can see that this is a principle that holds true everywhere in life. Whatever it is that you do, you'll find that adversity can prosper the soul, while prosperity can be adverse to it. That seems counterintuitive to us; we seek comfort and to avoid problems. It's right and proper that we do, as long as we understand what's happening within us as these circumstances play out.

It would be foolish to go chasing after problems and to avoid success—we'll see that Joseph didn't use that strategy. Instead, the secret is to praise God during the times of storm, and to double down on serving him during the sunny days. When times are good, we need to remind ourselves every day that we owe everything to God, who has given and who can always take away.

Joseph passed yet another test, refusing to lose his spiritual edge. Let's discover how we can learn from his example and keep growing while the sun is shining.

THE MYTH OF SUNSET

In this chapter, and nearly everywhere else, we throw around phrases such as "while the sun is shining." We speak of the sun rising, coming in, going out, and being brighter at some times than others. And of course, we're dead wrong!

A few centuries of science have taught us the truth about the sun: It never goes anywhere. It doesn't rise, set, or trudge across the sky; *we* are the ones who move.

But what's the difference? Why make an issue of simple semantics?

The sun is not God, as many pagan religions had it. But the sun can be an effective analogy for God and his blessings upon us. Just as we get the movements of the sun wrong, we tend to think God's love is shining down sometimes and not others. In reality, he is more constant than the sun, more eternal. His blessings never cease for an instant. Again, it is the world that turns, the world that blocks out our view of God.

The sun never rises or sets, but stays in its place and holds the world in orbit around it. God, in the same way, never goes anywhere. There is no shadow of turning with him, but we are constantly inconstant. We have many ways to block out his light.

As we speak about the "good times" and "tough times" in this book, we must never forget that *all* times under God are good, and that the light of the world is never extinguished.

"For the Lord God is a sun and shield; the Lord bestows favor and honor; no good thing does he withhold from those whose walk is blameless" (Psalm 84:11).

SUNSHINE STRATEGIES

1. Embrace the Blessings.

First, notice that Joseph doesn't blush shyly, say, "Aw, shucks," and turn down his big promotion. He takes on the job of his life, because he knows it is God he is truly serving, and not just Pharaoh. He understands that everything up to now has been designed to prepare him for this moment—and he embraces the blessing.

As a matter of fact, he embraces all the perks that come along with his job promotion. New threads? Check. Top-of-the-line chariot? Check. New wife? Bring it on! Humility isn't a role-playing exercise of blessing denial; it's knowing exactly who we are, no more and no less, and embracing the role we are given. Joseph accepted all the advantages he was offered, and proceeded to show the world how to use them rightly.

We've mentioned that it's difficult to be wealthy without being worldly. But this doesn't mean it's wrong to be wealthy, simply that we must carry that burden and be responsible for our godliness. Wealth and power, rightly used, can achieve wonderful things for God's kingdom. Proverbs 29:2 reads, "When the righteous thrive, the people rejoice." We don't need more Christians walking away from their influence—we need them better using it to glorify God.

When God blesses your life, accept those blessings wholeheartedly, and reflect their light back upon him.

2. Don't Let Up.

One of the most important principles of serving God during good times is simply to keep on keeping on. Joseph never rested on his laurels. He never said, "Well, I've paid my dues, and now I'm going to relax and let the good times roll."

Genesis 41:46–49 gives evidence of Joseph being as industrious as ever, if not more so. Like all the great leaders in the Scriptures, he was driven by a mission statement, a great task God had given him to accomplish. Jesus kept his sights on seeking and saving the lost; Paul on taking the gospel to the Gentiles; and Joseph on shepherding Egypt through an eventual famine. Notice the action words in this passage: He *went out*, he *traveled*, he *collected*, he *stored up*, and he *kept records*. Joseph was always on the move, knowing that he only had so much time to prepare the nation.

Most people have heard the expression, "Make hay while the sun shines." The saying is actually hundreds of years old. In the Middle Ages, before machinery, hay was much harder for farmers to produce. They needed lots of consistent heat to dry out the grass. So if there were sunny skies for an extended period, they knew they had to make hay while they had the opportunity. Once the wet weather came, no hay could be produced.

Joseph was rigorous in storing up grain during the "fat" years. There must have been some people who questioned it: "How do we really know that big drought is coming? Some guy had a dream—really?" Joseph kept everybody working and saving through the power and force of his leadership, and he also made his employer wealthy.

One of the best ways to keep your edge during good times is to keep doing what you've been doing. Work hard; it's good for the soul.

3. Stay Connected to People.

One of the reasons adversity is good for us is the way it forces us to connect with other people. When the storms come, we realize we can't get by alone. Success, on the other hand, can be very isolating. Many of the world's wealthiest people live like hermits. They believe that money means the ability to pull away from others and be independent. And the price of that philosophy is loneliness.

Not only did Joseph make his employer wealthy, but he worked hard to benefit others, too. Genesis 47 shows us that he used his skills not for his own benefit, but to help his community when times grew tough. It's also interesting to note that he made people pay for the grain that he dispensed, as the "fat" years gave way to the lean ones. We live in an age of entitlements, and as we read this chapter of Genesis we envision long welfare lines with grain handouts. But Joseph didn't do it that way. The grain was available, but people were required to give something for it. They gave money, then livestock, and eventually sold themselves as slaves when necessary. Joseph understood the principle that people need to earn their bread; otherwise they lose their dignity.

I was in the Smoky Mountains, at a picnic area, when I saw a sign that read, "Don't feed the bears." Most of us understand why: Animals easily grow dependent upon handouts. They forget how to care for themselves. Joseph followed God's principles as he cared for people. What seemed like strict policy actually worked for the love and betterment of society.

In an earlier chapter, we discussed how we need to connect with people when we're discouraged. We need to keep those connections strong during encouraging times, too. There is never a time when God wants us to stop interacting with and ministering to others.

4. Be Compassionate.

Joseph was industrious, profitable, ministry-driven, and even demanding. But he was also compassionate. We can't get involved in the needs of people without bonding with them and coming to love them. Joseph gave the people seeds so that they could begin planting for future prosperity. He only asked that when the crops came in, the people should give a fifth to Pharaoh; the rest would provide plenty to feed their families.

The people said, "You have saved our lives" (Genesis 47:25).

The deal Joseph offered was more than fair. It protected them through the worst of times and provided hope for the best of times. People were motivated to work hard to buy back their freedom, their land, their livestock, and their homes. Wealth and power didn't corrupt or isolate Joseph—they made him even more compassionate and more eager to serve others.

> **DURING** your sunny days, you'll appreciate the weather even more when you get involved in the needs of those who are encountering storms.

During your sunny days, you'll appreciate the weather even more when you get involved in the needs of those who are encountering storms. You won't lose your spiritual edge; you'll find yourself even closer to God as he fills your heart with compassion for the needs of people.

5. Keep a Grateful Heart.

Above all, it's clear that Joseph always gave thanks and glory to God. One of the most striking indications of this is the account of the two sons born to Joseph during the good years and before the famine arrived.

Joseph had taken an Egyptian wife and started a family—something always at the center of our lives during the sunny times. Two sons arrived, and Joseph glorified God through their names:

> *Joseph named his firstborn Manasseh and said, "It is because God has made me forget all my trouble and all my father's household." The second son he named Ephraim and said, "It is because God has made me fruitful in the land of my suffering."*
>
> —Genesis 41:51–52

The first name, Manasseh, had the literal meaning, *he who causes to forget*. As we'll see in the next chapter, Joseph would be tested one more time, and this name would represent the very basis of his testing. There's power in focusing on the good things God has done, and forgetting the misery that lies behind.

The second name, Ephraim, carried the meaning of *fertile land*. Again Joseph focused on what God was doing. But the fertility was more than grain. Joseph was now fulfilling the legacy of his great-grandfather, Abraham, whom God had promised a great nation. The children of Joseph and his brothers would multiply quickly in Egypt, forming the nation that God would call home to a land of promise.

6. Be Prepared for the Changing Seasons.

Joseph understood one truth quite clearly: Life can be turned inside out in the flicker of an instant. One moment you can be a young prince, a dreamer of dreams, and the next a lowly slave. One day you can be a forgotten prison inmate, and the next a prime minister. Life has its seasons, its cycles of storm and fair weather. The very essence of Joseph's great work was to help a nation use its sunny season to prepare for its days of dryness. He'd had long, dark days sitting in his prison, talking to God and planning for what he would do if he ever got to see another blue sky. I believe he committed himself to use that time well, if God blessed him with the opportunity. And when the time came, God honored his devotion.

Whatever season of life you're moving through right now, God is with you, and he is preparing you for another time, another opportunity. Neither tough times nor tender ones last forever. But the purposes of God are eternal. Jesus is a man for all seasons.

Paul wrote his young friend Timothy with advice on how to make hay while the sun is shining:

> *Command those who are rich in this present world not to be arrogant nor to put their hope in wealth, which is so uncertain, but to put their hope in God, who richly provides us with everything for our enjoyment. Command them to do good, to be rich in good deeds, and to be generous and willing to share. In this way they will lay up treasure for themselves as a firm foundation for the coming age, so that they may take hold of the life that is truly life.*
>
> —1 Timothy 6:17–19

Wealth can be used for God's kingdom, but it should never become our security. We can avoid that by giving thanks each day for the God who provides all blessings—and by being rich in good deeds, for doing so reminds us of what true wealth really is.

During one sunny summer recently, I was traveling through northern Ohio. I love getting off the interstates and driving down those scenic highways that show us the heartland of America. And what a lovely day it was. I passed a magnificent farm that was obviously blessed by God. The corn, as the song says, was as high as an elephant's eye. The bean fields looked ripe for the picking. Everything was well tended, and was bearing fruit in season.

I slowed down to enjoy taking in the sight of the kind of farm on which so much of our country came of age. The house was framed by a well-manicured yard and a white picket fence. The barns had a fresh coat of red paint. But what caught my eye was the towering silo, probably seventy feet high, on which I read this message:

TO GOD BE THE GLORY

While the sun is shining, make your hay. Build your farm and family. Enjoy every blessing God has given you, and make every one of them a monument to the greatness of our Lord.

QUESTIONS FOR YOU

1. If life has its seasons, what season are you living through right now? Why?

2. What factors make it so easy to forget God when times are easy?

3. What classic mistakes do people make as they grow comfortable, distancing them from God?

4. Why are other people such an important part of the experience of staying connected to God?

5. If you're in the midst of a "sunny" time, what practical steps will help you make the most of it this week?

10: WHEN THE BAD GUYS WIN

Why Won't God Punish the Wicked?

IT'S RIGHT OUTSIDE the passenger-side window, whenever you drive. And there's something creepy about it. Check the side mirror and you see these words:

> Objects in mirror are closer than they appear.

Did you know those words are there by federal decree? The law says they must be printed in letters 4.8 mm or larger. And if you've done much driving, you know it's a valid warning.

But why are the objects closer than they appear? It turns out your mirror is convex in order to offer a wider field of view. You see more of what's behind you, but you also lose a little depth perception.

The little "objects" wording makes an appearance in the movie *Jurassic Park.* A huge T-Rex is lumbering in pursuit of a jeep. The driver looks into his side mirror, and there's the warning—with a great, toothy face over it.

Sometimes the past seems to chase us down the road of life, and it's a closer and deeper threat than we realize. Have you ever known people who couldn't seem to outrun the past? Who held on to grudges for decades? Carl Ericsson was one of those.

Carl was seventy-three, a retired insurance salesman. He'd been married to his sweetheart for more than forty-four years. He had been successful in business and built a rewarding life. But in June 2012, he visited an old classmate named Norman Johnson. He rang the doorbell, lifted a gun, and shot Norman down.

Why? Fifty years earlier, Norman had placed an athletic supporter over Carl's head. It had happened in their high school locker room, and Carl had been humiliated. It was a traumatic memory for him. Half a century passed. Both men married, worked, and grew old. Then one day, Carl Ericsson suddenly realized he wanted to kill his old classmate.

Absolutely nobody saw it coming, least of all Carl himself. *Objects in mirror are closer than they appear.*

We've talked a lot about testing in this book. We've taken a case study of one man, tried severely over time by doubt, despair, appetite, and even by the temptation to be corrupted by success. We face all these ourselves. But there's one more test that comes a few miles down the road. It comes once you think you've put all that behind you.

This is another big one—it's going to determine your state of mind for the rest of your life. Can you come to terms with the past? In our next and final chapter, we'll discuss aging. The key to contentment in those years is to be at peace with the past.

We'll also find that, to be at peace with ourselves, we must be at peace with the acts of God. Do we see him as fair and just, to ourselves and to others? Some grow bitter because they feel they've gotten a raw deal, while others, less worthy, have prospered. Good things happen to bad people. Why?

So as we come to the homestretch in the life of Joseph, let's examine these issues: How do we make peace with the past—with our past, and God's past?

Let's find out how close those objects in the rearview mirror are. Joseph did.

WHEN WORLDS COLLIDE

I can never read the story of Joseph without wondering about his emotions. His life was so extraordinary; what a memoir he could have written. He knew he was a part of the line of Abraham, a line that would shape world history. But it seemed he had been chewed up and spat out by that legacy. His brothers, presumably, would build the Hebrew future while Joseph lived and died in a separate culture, as slave and prisoner and then as prime minister—but not as part of the legacy to which he was born.

Did he ever think of those brothers? Surely he did. Were there twinges of bitterness? We have no evidence of it, but it would have been understandable. And what about God? He'd been with Joseph. He'd had a vast plan, but why did it allow so many "bad guys" to get off?

Maybe he no longer thought about these things—he was incredibly busy now. Pharaoh had placed the survival of a great nation in his hands. And Joseph was "hands on," one of the great detailed minds of the Bible. His plan for coordinating the nation's grain store was comprehensive, and he had his hand in everything. So let's imagine that the past wasn't in his rearview mirror at all on that morning when he looked up and saw what he did.

There were ten familiar faces, staring at him in humility and deference.

The story is found in Genesis 42: "So when Joseph's brothers arrived, they bowed down to him with their faces to the ground" (Genesis 42:6). Joseph knew immediately who they were, even with years of change. All the pain had begun with a dream that painted this picture: his brothers as sheaves of grain, bowing before his sheaf. Now, here they were, bowing to ask for . . . *grain*.

Joseph played it cool. He was surely floored, unprepared for the emotional jolt. But he had other reasons for not coming clean. Before knowing how to proceed, he needed to test his brothers. Still, imagine the emotions running riot within him. The old, bitter world had broken into the new and hopeful one. His past had overtaken him; the past was closer than he'd realized.

The brothers didn't know him. He was nothing like the scrawny, pampered seventeen-year-old they once knew. This was an impressive man at midlife, a regal and powerful figure in his prime. Joseph, they believed, was long dead. So he held the advantage, and he decided he would use it.

Here were the tempting thoughts he must have faced: *Boom! Revenge is sweet . . . They've got this coming to 'em . . . Why not show them the mercy they showed me?*

Remember, grace wasn't the coin of the realm in ancient practice. An eye for an eye was the norm, and you gave people what they earned. So we can't come to this narrative with Christianized expectations. Nearly anyone in Joseph's place would be expected to even the score. That was the righteous way of things.

DREAMS AND SCHEMES

Joseph held all the cards, and he weighed his options.

He could arrest his brothers as spies and have them executed.

He could reveal his true identity, then send them home to Jacob empty-handed.

He could even take the high road—tell them who he was, rub in the guilt, give them a bit of grain, and send them off with their tails between their legs.

But Joseph also had a thousand questions that needed answering. Was his father alive? How was Benjamin, now grown up? Had his brothers changed? Was there still some possibility of getting his family back?

So he played for time. He took them prisoner, accusing them of being spies. One of them would be allowed to go home and bring back their little brother, whom they had described. It would prove their sincerity, he explained. He was testing his brothers—and himself.

Joseph needed time to work it all out. He was a careful, deliberate, detailed man, and he knew God was at work here. Yet before there could be reconciliation, he needed to know if his brothers had truly changed. Forgiveness is a gift, but trust must be earned.

He wanted information about his family, and to see Benjamin again. And there's another factor at play here. Could it be that he received just a bit of satisfaction from watching his brothers squirm—that he couldn't resist twisting the knife a little? Once, he had been sent with a message to his brothers, and they accused him of being a spy for their father. Now the sandal was on the other foot—they were the spies, and they were in prison.

I also like to think that Joseph was thinking of his old dream. *Eleven* sheaves had bowed, but there were only ten brothers here. Benjamin would make eleven, and since God gave the dream, the picture needed completion.

On the third day, Joseph told the brothers he had changed his mind. Everyone but one could go home, he'd keep a hostage, and he still expected to see Benjamin; no grain unless he met this youngest brother. Simeon was tied up and kept in prison.

It's here that we learn what was going on inside the brothers' heads. Joseph, who knew their language, was able to listen in and hear this:

> *Surely we are being punished because of our brother. We saw how*
> *distressed he was when he pleaded with us for his life, but we*
> *would not listen; that's why this distress has come upon us. . . .*
> *Now we must give an accounting for his blood.*
> —Genesis 42:21–22

Ah, now that's interesting! It brings us squarely back to the act of God we're exploring in this chapter: Why does he allow evil to prosper? We seldom consider the consuming punishment of personal guilt.

179

JUDGMENT FROM WITHIN

People have always seen the prosperity of those who seem evil, and asked, "What's that all about? Isn't God paying attention?"

Asaph, in Psalm 73, confesses,

> *I envied the arrogant*
> *when I saw the prosperity of the wicked.*
> *They have no struggles;*
> *their bodies are healthy and strong.*
> *They are free from common human burdens;*
> *they are not plagued by human ills.*
>
> —Psalm 73:3–5

That's certainly how it appears, at least. But how much of this is our imagination? We can imagine Joseph thinking, *My brothers went on their merry way after selling me off. I bet they've been healthy and happy, growing older with our father.*

Bitterness is a skillful liar; it paints all kinds of excruciating pictures with the aim of increasing our anguish. Here Asaph believes the wicked don't even get sick. But what goes on *inside* people? Notice what the brothers say here. They connect an Egyptian stranger's harshness to something that happened twenty years ago or more: "We are being punished because of our brother" (Genesis 42:21).

WE CAN'T fool our own hearts. We can't fool God.

Guilt has been consuming them all these years. We shouldn't assume that nonbelievers don't feel the pain of guilty conscience. God has placed within all of us a sense of our own sin, and one of the silent but deadly ways we are disciplined is through the relentlessness of the human conscience.

Why do the wicked prosper? The first answer is that we don't know everything, but we do know evil brings no inner contentment; much the reverse instead.

I always loved that story by Edgar Allen Poe, "The Telltale Heart." A man commits the perfect crime—a murder without evidence. But his heart convicts him, and he can't sleep at night. All he hears is the thumping of his victim's heart. And of course, nobody hears it but himself, because it is generated by his soul. We can't fool our own hearts. We can't fool God.

The conscience is a complex thing. It appears on no X-ray, but we all know it's there. Paul speaks of people "whose consciences have been seared as with a hot iron" (1 Timothy 4:2). Their sin becomes so ingrained that they can no longer feel anything. Jeremiah describes those so steeped in sin that they "do not even know how to blush" (Jeremiah 8:12). Those people are heading for their own destruction. But most people indeed have a moral compass, which is the first line of defense against a life of disobedience.

Whatever Joseph assumed about his brothers, it's clear that they knew they'd done something terribly wrong, and that there were spiritual consequences. Jacob hadn't found them out, and they thought they'd committed the perfect crime. But as soon as they found themselves in a fix, they said, "We're being punished." How many times had they said or thought that in these two-plus decades? How much dread had they labored under? How many nights did they lie awake in those earlier years, wondering what would happen if Joseph escaped and walked in the door? Would Jacob disinherit them?

After Cain murdered Abel, he told God,

My punishment is more than I can bear. Today you are driving me from the land, and I will be hidden from your presence; I will be a restless wanderer on the earth, and whoever finds me will kill me.

—Genesis 4:13–14

Guilt is a powerful compulsion—part of God's punishment, and some would say the hardest part of it—but not all of God's punishment. We need to remember that not every form of discipline is open to view.

YOU WOULDN'T BELIEVE IT

Habakkuk was an Old Testament prophet who posed this question to God:

> *Why do you make me look at injustice?*
> *Why do you tolerate wrongdoing?*
> *Destruction and violence are before me;*
> *there is strife, and conflict abounds.*
> *Therefore the law is paralyzed,*
> *and justice never prevails.*
> *The wicked hem in the righteous,*
> *so that justice is perverted.*
>
> —Habakkuk 1:3–4

And here is God's answer:

> *Look at the nations and watch—*
> *and be utterly amazed.*
> *For I am going to do something in your days*
> *that you would not believe,*
> *even if you were told.*
>
> —Habakkuk 1:5

Then God begins to reveal what he's about to do—and Habakkuk is indeed astounded. The Babylonians are going to rise up and "sweep across the whole earth" (v. 6). This happened, of course, but nobody expected it.

As we look back on our own lives, we can often agree that if God had briefed us in advance, we wouldn't believe what was coming. Yet he always has a plan, and his plans are perfect, and they're rarely what anyone sees coming.

Joseph would have struggled to believe, as a boy, that he would be a slave and a prisoner and a world leader. His brothers might not have accepted, when they went to Egypt to beg, that they would move in with their brother Joseph, who ran things there, and come home much later by walking across the Red Sea.

Secondly, then, when sin appears to go unpunished, we need to remember that we only see a small bit of the picture—in time and in space. God moves in mysterious ways—but he moves in power, and ultimately in justice.

Jeremiah has a rather polite way of posing the same thorny question: "You are always righteous, LORD, when I bring a case before you. Yet I would speak with you about your justice: Why does the way of the wicked prosper? Why do all the faithless live at ease?" (Jeremiah 12:1). It's fascinating that this is a frequently asked question of prophets to God. Again, God answers Jeremiah in broad terms, citing nations and epochs. All of this points up the fact that we are prisoners of the moment. We see ourselves, and our little circles. We know nothing of the vast canvas on which our Creator is painting.

More often than not, grossly sinful people get their just rewards fairly quickly anyway. If we would just give it a little time, we'd see. "Your sin will find you out." But even if we never see it, we must trust that our God is faithful to his promises, and that he is just.

There is a very old saying: "The wheels of God grind slowly, but they grind exceedingly fine." It's the word picture of a mill that churns away. At first glance there's nothing impressive to see, but the big wheel keeps on turning, and the wicked keep losing the war, even if they win a few battles. The most important explanation for the seeming prosperity of the wicked is that we spend this life gazing through imperfect glass. Objects in the mirror are closer to justice than they appear. He is not deceived.

COULD WE HAVE IT WRONG?

There's something else to consider. Not only are we limited in time perspective but by bias. The best way I could show you this principle would be to take you with me to a game. It doesn't matter what kind of game. You name the sport. One thing they all have in common is that *nobody* is satisfied by the officiating. You never walk back to the parking lot and hear people say, "Weren't the referees just great? Those were some of the *fairest* calls I've seen." We dress our kids in team colors, not black-and-white striped tops and whistles.

In basketball, people leap from their seats and call out, "Whaddaya doing, ref? He mugged him!" In football, it's, "Hey, ref, how is that *not* interference?" In baseball, it's, "Are you blind, ump?"

If you want to be reminded of the imperfections of humanity, sports is your venue. No matter whether we're in a stadium or a sanctuary, our judgment often leaves something to be desired. We all want to see the rules followed (particularly to our personal benefit). And we're all experts who are eager to give the universe's Referee the benefit of our guidance.

If you've been to those coliseums or stadiums or ballparks, you've noticed that vocal fans are driven more by emotion than clear observation. We all tend to see the situations in which the rules should work in our favor, and to deemphasize the ones that hold us to task.

It's another factor we need to consider when we question God about what he allows. Do we really know the hearts of other people? Yes, there are occasions when it's clear that evil may be prospering for the moment. The celebrity gets away with murder. The movie star lives a public life of immorality and only becomes more popular. But for the most part, righteous living brings natural rewards, and sin is self-punishing now, even before God's judgment comes. It's not so much that we break God's laws, but we break ourselves upon them. (See "It's the Law" below.)

Given these considerations, we should live humbly before God and one another, drawing as few conclusions as possible about who should or shouldn't be punished. But one more factor here, and it's the most important of all for us. We need to take care that we protect our own hearts against bitterness in the face of wickedness.

Joseph, once again, is our example.

IT'S THE LAW

The British mystery writer Dorothy Sayers once explained that there are two kinds of laws: the law of the stop sign and the law of the fire.

Stop signs have to do with laws set by *people*. An intersection is dangerous, so we put up a sign. We set fines for those who fail to stop. But the authorities can increase the fine if too many accidents continue; or they can remove the sign if the situation dictates. People can also run the stop sign at night without consequences. It's a human law, and only humans will enforce it.

The law of fire, on the other hand, says that if you put your hand in a fire, it will be burned. Even if we all vote not to be burned, the fire is still going to do its thing. This law isn't made by humanity. It's enforced by the laws of physics, and as such, carries its own punishment.

The point is that we often confuse *human* laws with *God's* laws. His laws are more like fire. They are self-enforcing; punishment comes installed. This is why "you may be sure that your sin will find you out" (Numbers 32:23).

GOD INTENDED IT FOR GOOD

When the brothers returned with their youngest brother, Joseph really set things in motion. The story is told in Genesis 43–44. He invited them all to dinner, and arranged their seats in order of the brothers' ages—Joseph mastering the details as usual. This unsettled the brothers: How did he know such a thing?

He had also set them up to look like thieves, planting their silver (the payment for the grain) back in their sacks. This would give them something to worry about upon returning, testing their courage. Would they keep their word to return if it was dangerous to do so?

But the brothers didn't waver. It had taken a great deal of convincing for Jacob to finally allow Benjamin to make the trip, and the brothers proved their growth. God, we find, had been acting within them, too. Again we see just how little we really know from watching the outside of things—God is at work all the time, molding and shaping people.

Joseph "forgave" the brothers for the silver that had mysteriously reappeared in their bags. It had done its work; they had boldly come back to plead their innocence and bring Benjamin with them. Nor could Joseph remain so cool and calculating—not after he set eyes on Benjamin after all these years. He had to leave the room to hide the tears that flooded his eyes.

Still, there was one final test. A silver cup was placed in Benjamin's travel bag, and an inspection made him appear guilty. For the brothers, this would be absolutely the worst-case scenario, since Jacob had so much dreaded risking his youngest. From Joseph's perspective, the way was clear to keep his beloved brother as a "slave" and send the rest home. Many would have considered this to be reasonable justice for everyone. The brothers would get their just deserts, and Benjamin, who had done nothing to Joseph, could stay and live the royal life.

But Joseph was still sifting the character of his half-brothers. And now, he was touched when Judah offered his own life in exchange for Benjamin's freedom. Such an act stood in bold contrast with how Joseph had been treated, so many years ago. Judah doesn't say, "Our father will kill us if we come home without Benjamin." He says, "Do not let me see the misery that would come on my father" (Genesis 44:34).

Judah had, in effect, spared Joseph's life all those years before, by urging that the boy be sold. But his reasons then had come from greed; there was no profit in simple murder. These decades later, Judah was a different man.

Joseph then came clean with them; he simply couldn't control his emotions any longer. In one of the Bible's most touching scenes, he sent away the Egyptians, so that only the sons of Jacob would be in the room, and he said, "I am Joseph!" (Genesis 45:3). His brothers were speechless, and Joseph said, "Come closer to me."

And listen to what he said: "And now, do not be distressed and do not be angry with yourselves for selling me here, because it was to save lives that God sent me ahead of you" (Genesis 45:5). Joseph saw all of life from a heavenly perspective. It made the difference in everything that happened to him, how others saw him, how he responded. Later, he put it this way: "You intended to harm me, but God intended it for good to accomplish what is now being done, the saving of many lives" (Genesis 50:20).

This is the Old Testament version of Romans 8:28: God uses all things for his good purposes, even when we intended them for our bad purposes. The saving of many lives is the great theme of God, and it should be our great theme as well. It's all about God's unfailing love for his world—ultimately, nothing else matters but the reconciliation he wants to make with us and among us.

Yes, Joseph had an incredible capacity for avoiding bitterness, because he was humble before the purposes of the Lord. As it transformed his attitude, so should it transform ours.

THE CHALLENGE OF GRACE

We look at the family of Jacob and see so much dysfunction from the beginning. But observe the happy ending, as elderly Jacob uproots the family estate and everyone settles happily in Egypt. Grace works miracles. If Joseph had been like most people, he would have evened the score, and this story would have had a sour ending. But it doesn't, and that's because someone was willing to view life and relationships in the way God sees them.

What about your life? Are you practicing amazing grace or a maddening grudge? What if you took a relationship inventory of the people in your life? How many have wronged you? How many of them have you forgiven? Believe me, grace and forgiveness are more than antiquated Bible stories. They are strategies for bringing true joy, peace, and contentment to your life. I could give you so many examples, but try this one.

Frank and Elizabeth Morris of Hopkinsville, Kentucky, got the worst of all possible news. It was Christmas of 1982, and their son Ted had perished in an automobile accident. When they learned that it came at the hands of a drunk driver, one Tommy Pigage—a self-described "hoodlum"—who walked away from the crash without a scratch, they were furious. How could God allow such a thing? No pious platitudes or recited Bible verses could give them comfort; their faith was devastated.

Ted, their child, had been a model college student, a devout young Christian whom everyone admired, and obviously on the fast track toward a life of service and honor. Now some thoughtless drunk had put an end to all that, and hadn't even picked up a bruise for his efforts.

The Morrises became consumed by the idea of justice. Everyone who knew the Morrises sympathized with them. The loss of a child, in such an egregious manner, is the deepest blow life can offer. And why shouldn't we expect the wicked to receive their due punishment?

Tommy Pigage received a suspended sentence, a slap on the wrist, so to speak. Ted's parents were beyond outraged; they couldn't let it all go. Their lives began to revolve around monitoring the activities of Pigage. Their goal was to catch him in some lawless situation that would finally be his downfall. He would rot in prison or they would die waiting for it.

Sure enough, a few months passed, and Pigage picked up a second charge of public drunkenness. He went back to jail.

But once it happened, Elizabeth Morris didn't feel the sense of jubilation she had expected. Nothing but emptiness. And for the first time in a long while, she took a good look at herself, and reflected on her faith in Christ. How did Christ feel about all this anger she had harbored? She knew it was eating her away from the inside out like an emotional cancer.

Tommy Pigage couldn't have been too hopeful when he was informed that someone named Elizabeth Morris was there to see him. But the meeting was a shocker. She came back later with her husband Frank. The talk was calm; open. Regret was discussed; forgiveness was offered. It all led to Tommy being invited into the home of the Morrises. They legally adopted the man who had killed their son.

One night, they all attended a meeting of Mothers Against Drunk Driving. On the way home, the conversation became more spiritual and personal. At 10:00 p.m. they stopped at a small church, and Frank, a former part-time minister, baptized Tommy Pigage. Forgiveness, mercy, grace, and the love of God had won out over bitterness. How could we ever let there be a different ending?

Every human story should end in reconciliation.

BREAKING THE CYCLE

William Faulkner said, "The past is never dead. In fact, it's not even past." You may think you can put things behind without coming to terms with them—but you can't.

In the South, there's a strange ivy known as kudzu. It grows along the highways, climbs trees and fences, and consumes everything in its path. It was first introduced to the region in 1886, imported from Japan as a kind of ornamental shrub. But it is currently claiming 150,000 new acres annually. They say that when kudzu gets onto your property, the first year it sleeps; the second, it creeps; the third it leaps.

That's a kind of metaphor for the anger in our world today. People don't even realize the bitterness they're holding in. But it sleeps for a while, then it creeps, then finally it leaps—we just snap, and we don't know why. Ask Carl Ericsson, the quiet retiree who shot a man for humiliating him fifty years earlier. Worst of all, the people who are victims of our anger aren't even the ones who put it there. So we just perpetuate the cycle, spread the virus of bitterness and rage. Yet every time we forgive, the angels celebrate; Satan loses another acre of this world.

Forgiveness doesn't come easily; it can be the hardest work of all. It requires the right mindset, the right humility, and the most powerful of wills. Above all, we can't forgive without the power of God animating us. Joseph teaches us three strong principles, however, to get us started.

• First, forgiveness means releasing my right to retaliate.

That's why it's difficult. Human nature is stimulus/response, cause and effect. I do unto you because you did unto me.

But forgiveness isn't me pretending what you did was right; it's not me saying I wasn't hurt or even that it doesn't matter. It's just saying, "I'm going to let it go."

Joseph told the brothers they had intended him harm. But acknowledging that God had other intentions, he could let it go. He could be free to break the cycle of grief and leave the justice to God.

Romans 12:19 says, "Do not take revenge, my dear friends, but leave room for God's wrath, for it is written: 'It is mine to avenge; I will repay,' says the Lord." We're saying, "Lord—this one is yours."

And there's an odd feeling when you cross over that line of the will from anger to grace. You expect it to be frustrating, but instead you feel a tremendous load off your shoulders. Bitter people are the ones carrying all the baggage.

I've seen this in my friends, the Becketts of Knoxville, Tennessee. Their daughter died representing Jesus as a missionary volunteer in Afghanistan, gunned down by terrorists. Cheryl gave her life trying to share the gospel, and her parents were overwhelmed with grief. But when I asked Charles Beckett if he felt bitter, he said, "No, I can't hate the people my daughter gave her life to reach. And already I see God using the evil in this situation. He didn't *cause* it, but he'll *use* it. Cheryl didn't give her life in vain."

Do Charles and Mary Beckett have the *right* to bitterness? By human tradition, yes. But who wants to cling to a right that affords nothing but pain? Why not align ourselves with the kingdom of God, which always wins in the end?

• Second, forgiveness means taking action toward restoration.

I'm sure this isn't exciting news, either—not when we first hear it. We could at least get a little bittersweet satisfaction out of saying, "Yeah, I forgive you. Now get out of my life."

But we live a resurrection faith, and that means we won't leave anything dead. All things are made new. We don't settle for détente, but push for full-scale reconciliation. The deepest and most satisfying relationships in life come when God has put something back together that seemed completely broken. But God won't make that happen unless we cooperate. And there must be two sides who are willing.

Joseph did everything right. He gave his brothers the opportunity to show repentance and to demonstrate how far they had come. He didn't pretend they hadn't terribly hurt him, but he let God effect full restoration among them.

- **Third, forgiveness means letting God be God.**

The key to letting go of bitterness is seeing the world as God sees it. You might be angry at the man who stepped on your toe, until you realize he was blind. That changes things, doesn't it? When you see people as God sees them, you notice the blindness. You see lost, stumbling children who get caught up in this terrible cycle of anger, retaliating because no one has shown them another way.

As followers of Christ, we know that other way. We know the cure; we fight anger with love:

> *Do not repay anyone evil for evil. . . . If it is possible, as far as it depends on you, live at peace with everyone. Do not take revenge, my dear friends, but leave room for God's wrath.*
>
> —Romans 12:17–19

No, it's not easy to live by grace. But it's liberating. And once you've gotten a taste of it, you'll never want to be ruled by anger again.

As for the wicked, maybe they prosper—for a while. We simply trust God to make things right. The adventure of grace doesn't really give us time to think about such things. After all, God has forgiven us. He has released his right to retaliate and has reached out to restore us to himself. Knowing that, how can we remain bitter about anything or anyone?

QUESTIONS FOR YOU

1. What makes bitterness such a particularly powerful temptation?

2. How does guilt function as a form of divine discipline?

3. What are the limitations of our perspective, as we look upon God's dealings with others?

4. Which of the three directives for forgiveness do you find most challenging? Why?

5. Think of one person you need to forgive. How will you begin this week to move toward letting go of your grudge? Who can pray with you toward this end?

11: PARDON OUR DUST

Why Must Aging Be Such a Trial?

I LOVED MY MOTHER, and I struggled to watch her grow old. She had Alzheimer's in her final years—a prospect of dread for all of us, and for those we love. It's one of those cruel, incurable ailments that is no respecter of persons, in any sense. It steals away our identities, memory by memory. President Reagan had it. My mother had it.

Her care facility was an eight-hour drive from my home, as things worked out, so it took some extra diligence for me to spend time with her. Then, of course, with all the traveling, the reality of the visits could be devastating. I'd go to see her with a big smile, and with each visit she had slipped further away. Toward the end, she simply had no idea who I was. I would reminisce with her, gently hold her hand, and I'd think, *I'm just talking to myself. What are the chances she's still in there somewhere, listening, simply unable to get through?*

And on the way home, I would hash it out with God. I knew he could handle my frustration and my questions. "Why can't my mom be like so many of her friends, gracious and sharp and wise?" I would ask. I knew my Bible verses: "The glory of young men is their strength, and gray hair the splendor of the old" (Proverbs 20:29). So how splendorous is that gray hair when the mind beneath it fades into the distance? What is God up to?

I continued my visits, not from some sense of legalistic duty but because I loved my mother. I was losing a little more of her with each visit, but I could still look at her and remember who she had been in my life. I could honor her and give her my love, even if I received so little in return. Isn't that the essence of New Testament devotion?

Meanwhile, through these journeys I was brought to terms with my own mortality. There was no doubt about it: I was growing older, like every other member of the human race. The world around me seemed younger and more distant from my generation every day. My old body, once trim and athletic, was wearing down. And I wanted to ask God why it is that so much of our wisdom comes as we lose the energy to employ it.

> **I WAS** losing a little more of her with each visit, but I could still look at her and remember who she had been in my life.

God had a lot to teach me on these trips to see my mother. But he had a couple of miracles waiting for me, too. And that's your incentive to finish this chapter and find out what I mean.

Let's take a final look at the life of Joseph, as well as in the mirror, and find out what God is doing through the rigors of the aging process.

GOLDEN YEARS, GOLDEN FEARS

Age, like death, brings out the euphemisms in us—that's how we know we've come to a subject that makes people squirm. We airbrush the terminology.

Just as people don't die, but "pass away" or "go to their reward," nobody *gets old*; they become "eighty years young," or they're "seniors," as if back for one more year of high school. We say, "You're as old as you feel!" and, "Age is just a number!" We call them "golden" years, but if we're truthful, we'll admit they can feel more like tinfoil. And when we laugh and joke at the birthday parties of aging friends, aren't we whistling past the graveyard just a bit?

The truth is, no matter what we say, no matter how we couch the phrase, nobody really wants to get old. And for some foolish reason, we never quite expect to. Aging happens while we're making other plans, and it comes out of nowhere. How did we get to be thirty? That's *ancient*, we insist. Yet forty is breathing right down its neck, and one day we find ourselves attending our thirtieth high school reunion and thinking, "What happened to all these people? They're all so *old*!"

It's odd that so many characters of the Bible failed to age well, yet this is one more indication that our Bible is a book of truth:

- Moses grew spiritually with the years until an act of terrible judgment cost him the chance to enter the Promised Land.
- David, the greatest and the most gifted of kings, finally found something he couldn't do well: lead a family.
- Solomon was the wisest of all men until he grew soft on idol worship.
- And Jacob, the father of Joseph, isn't the most gracious of granddads, as we'll see.

If aging is a test, a lot of those people, heroes though they were, struggled to pass it. Someone said that the tough thing about life is that it's so daily. Well, the tough thing about growing old is that it's so final. There is no gear for reverse; no do-overs. Aging never takes a day off. But as Maurice Chevalier said, growing old is not so bad when you consider the alternative. And if you actually know who Maurice Chevalier was—well, you get the idea.

Most of us have seen other people take on the years with minimal grace, and it's not a pretty sight. Some men and women, emotionally unprepared, make terrible mistakes in their doomed quest to tell themselves they're still young. They have affairs. They make ill-advised investments. Or they simply grow sad and bitter.

Then again, we've seen some people take the other fork in the road. Their golden years actually *shine*. They seem to grow stronger, wiser, and more content, as if they actually prefer senior status to youth. You wonder how they do it, because they seem so sincere in the appearance of enjoying the autumn years of life.

You might say that faith separates the men from the boys, and the women from the girls, when it comes to growing older. Do you really, sincerely believe that you're heading for a new life beyond this earthly horizon, and that it will be vastly superior to this world in every way?

If you do believe that, with all your heart, what exactly do you fear? What is the source of the dread? Why do you fear death at all, and clutch this fading, imperfect life so frantically?

It's only human to fear the unknown, of course, but at some point, genuine trust in God should make a difference. We should be able to say, "I love my life, and I don't particularly enjoy accumulating birthdays; I'm not into the rheumatism, exactly. But I'm excited about what lies ahead. I'm going to a place where every tear has dried, where there's nothing but joy, and where I'm looking forward to the ultimate family reunion. Forgive me if I smile just a little, knowing that heaven is so close I can taste it."

OLDIES BUT GOODIES

Virgil Thomas, my father-in-law, lived to be ninety. I've never seen anyone age as masterfully and attractively as he did. With each year, he was more fun to be with, more positive, more generous. There was a sense of joy in him as he focused on making others happy. And then, when we came to that moment when my wife worried about him living in his house alone—the expected argument never happened. He seemed to read our minds, and he smiled and said, "You know what? I've been thinking I'm tired of this old house. I think I might sell it and move into a retirement center. What do the two of you think?"

His three children shared a sigh of relief. But why should they have expected anything different? Virgil had proven to be ready for each new season as he entered it. He sold his car before anyone had to take away his car keys. When he got to the extended care facility, he acted as if it were the Ritz-Carlton, bragging on the food and claiming he had plenty of visitors. He said that now he had more time for his grandchildren, and he found ways to share his resources with them.

And as the shadow of death began to take form, he was honest and practical about it. His trust was in God, and he was ready to wake up to a fresh dawn in a land with no darkness. He was at peace with past, present, and future, and that's a recipe for old-age contentment.

Virgil Thomas was Exhibit A in the advanced course on graceful aging, and I would venture that you've known a Virgil or two in your own life. I learned a great deal from him, and I was humbled as I faced my own initial thoughts on this enigma of aging. In Christ, all things are possible. He promised to give us an abundant life, and he never put an expiration date on that.

Yet I have to be honest in my observation that the Virgils of the world are the exception to the rule. In too many cases, I've seen negative emotions of every kind. People seem to understand youth as something they have an entitlement to clutch. Aging is the enemy, death is an obscenity, and they will not go gently into that dark night. That's why plastic surgery has become a gold-mine industry. Tummy tucks, hair transplantation, face-lifts, Botox treatments—few want to look their age.

The truth is that no one in the history of the world has dodged the aging process, and it's not going to happen for you or me, either. Life is served out one day at a time, no more, no less, and it's a straight line from womb to tomb. We know the rules. Even the Bible says, in any number of places, that this life is but a mist that appears for a while, then vanishes.

That reality would be so disappointing, so pointless, if we didn't possess the promise of something very special on the far side of the grave; if we didn't see our lives as acts of God, with definite purposes and certain fulfillment.

Revelation 2:10 offers a promise from the mouth of Christ: "Be faithful, even to the point of death, and I will give you the crown of life." Some time ago I was given a plaque that simply reads, "Finish Strong." And those two words mean a great deal to me. This life is indeed a race—the New Testament writers offered that analogy more than once—and therefore we ought to approach it like marathon runners, chins down, legs pumping, straining with every fiber toward that finish line, because we know that a crown of glory waits for us there.

I heard about an elderly woman who brought levity to her church through her vibrant wit. After one of her typical quips, a younger woman gave her a little hug and said, "Madge, you're beautiful!"

Madge replied, "Well, I ought to be, honey—I'm eighty-five years old!" That's a perfectly straightforward statement. In Christ, we *ought* to be beautiful by the time we reach our later years. He's had a lot of time to transform us into his image. If they'll know we are Christians by our love, I submit that they should also know we are Christians by the grace of our aging.

OLD YET? TEST YOURSELF!

Author and pastor Greg Laurie, with tongue in cheek, offers us a quick examination to determine whether we've gotten old yet:

- You know you're getting old when you sink your teeth into a big, juicy steak—and they stay there.

- You know you're getting old when you dim the lights for economic reasons, not romantic ones.

- You know you're getting old when you've owned clothes for so long they've come back into style twice.

- You know you're getting old when you sing along to elevator music.

- You know you're getting old when you quit trying to hold your stomach in no matter who walks in the room.

Source: Greg Laurie, "God's Cure for Heart Trouble," *Preaching Today* Audio Issue no. 282.

THE LONG AND WINDING ROAD

We've followed the amazing saga that was Joseph's life. We've seen the various tests he faced, and examined how God was acting in each one.

Now we come to what could be the anticlimax. In dramatic terms, every story has "rising action," a climax, and then "falling action" toward the end of the tale. Clearly, Joseph's climactic experience was his opportunity to save a nation—topped by an emotional reunion with his family, resolving the conflicts that had existed with his brothers. What could be left?

F. Scott Fitzgerald once observed that there were "no second acts in American lives." And General Douglas MacArthur said in his farewell address that "old soldiers never die; they just fade away." Those observations reflect the fear we all have that at some point we come to the top of the hill, and the rest of the trip is all downhill. The fickle world will forget us, turning its attention to the next generation of young, attractive people.

Perhaps Joseph had come to that crisis moment when he thought that his great adventures had run out. Not that he could have complained—all the ingredients for "happily ever after" were in place. He had a position of power and honor, and his extended family was on its way to join him. But Joseph must have wondered what acts of God remained for him. Were there any more twists in his long and winding road?

From Genesis 46, we see that he actually had many more years ahead of him. He was forty, and he would live to the ripe old age of a hundred and ten—seventy more years, another lifetime, if a quieter one.

> *When they arrived in the region of Goshen, Joseph had his chariot made ready and went to Goshen to meet his father Israel. As soon as Joseph appeared before him, he threw his arms around his father and wept for a long time.*
>
> *Israel said to Joseph, "Now I am ready to die, since I have seen for myself that you are still alive."*
>
> —Genesis 46:28–30

Israel, of course, is Jacob's special name. In Genesis 32, we learn how he wrestled with a messenger from God through the night, and received a new name. The nation that rose from this family would bear that same name, for his children would define the twelve tribes.

Joseph was clearly thrilled to see his father after all these years—neither had known whether the other was even alive, and now they were reunited. There were tears, and Jacob remarks that now he can die a happy man. The loss of Joseph has tormented him for years.

If you read closely, you'll conclude that Jacob brings up his death perhaps a little too often. We've all known elderly relatives who developed a morbid approach: "This will be my last Thanksgiving; I won't be around to trouble you much longer." On the old TV show *Sanford and Son,* Fred Sanford was a caricature of this affectation. He would try to manipulate others by grabbing his heart and talking to his wife in heaven: "Elizabeth, this is the big one! It won't be much longer—I'm coming to join you!"

As we age, we feel a loss of power and influence. If we're not cautious, we find ourselves trading on the sympathies or guilt of those around us. It's a way to get attention or win an argument. We want "an aging grace." The Bible tells us to rejoice always, to be wise and loving rather than demanding. But the worst of human nature pulls us in another direction.

Florence Nightingale was the beloved English nurse of the nineteenth century, the "lady with the lamp" who would make the midnight rounds, going from tent to tent to care for wounded soldiers. She strengthened countless other sufferers, but there came a time when she was the one who needed encouragement. At fifty-six she was bedridden, certain she was on a collision course with death from heart disease. Now *she* was the patient. While she shut down her life and waited for death, thirty-four more years went by! She held on until she was ninety.

> **IT TURNS** out that in the kingdom economy, there are *plenty* of second acts among the saints.

Have you ever known someone like that, so focused on aches and pains that they took themselves out of the battle? Time is precious in every season of life. Jacob was "ready to die" once he saw Joseph—except that he had another seventeen years left to live. An aging grace lives life to the fullest, and lets God decide when the curtains are going to close. It's not ours to decide when the acts of God are complete for us. As a matter of fact, he is always doing surprising, remarkable things through older people. It turns out that in the kingdom economy, there are *plenty* of second acts among the saints. We need to be living life to the fullest, even as we age.

Joseph surely forgave his father's attitudes. He was gracious and loving with him, taking him in, helping him acclimate to a new home. Joseph's loving behavior is our first observation about the right way to grow old.

FAMILY FIRST

Second, we find that Joseph still honored his family, even though he had become a man of stature in an utterly different culture.

Genesis 46:31–34 tells how Joseph eased the way for his relatives to maintain their lifestyle in a new world. He assured his brothers that he'd go to Pharaoh and explain that they were herdsmen—*not* specifically shepherds. This requires a bit of explanation.

In Egyptian culture, shepherds were despised. There are various theories as to why this may have been so, but the point was that Joseph's family *could* be an embarrassment to him. He might well have told them, "I'm an important man. You all need to find some other line of work, so you don't disgrace my name."

But that didn't happen. Joseph was determined not only to have his family around him, but to give them the kind of life they had always enjoyed. So he briefed them carefully. He told them to simply tell Pharaoh, "We tend livestock." Unfortunately, his brothers couldn't handle that assignment. They told Pharaoh they were shepherds, and asked for the land of Goshen for tending their flocks. It's a tribute to the ruler's esteem of Joseph that Pharaoh granted their request.

Then, when Joseph introduced his father (Genesis 47:7–10), Jacob whined a little about his age and his troubles. He said that he was 130, and his years had been "few and difficult." He said this, of course, after miraculously recovering his son and avoiding starvation for the whole family. He had won the lottery and stood before a king, but he was complaining. It's all in how we look at things, but again, Pharaoh was kind.

All of this might have embarrassed Joseph to some extent—his brothers' coarseness, his father's whining. There was a great cultural gap between Egypt and Canaan, but Joseph formed a bridge between the two kinds of people. He was an ambassador of God's universal love.

What really mattered to Joseph was the opportunity to have an extended family once again, and particularly to be with his aging father. As Genesis 47 continues, we see that Joseph was by his father's side when Jacob was dying. Jacob requested a burial back home, in the land of his forefathers, and Joseph promised he would see that done.

Joseph traveled over to Goshen to visit his aging father just as I did with my mother. I wonder if he faced some of the same emotions. They'd been apart for all those years, and his father was fading. Maybe some part of Joseph found the past to be painful; certainly he was a busy man who was involved in all the details of his national work. But he found time for his father.

OFFERING THE BLESSING

God did something significant. At the beginning of Genesis 48, we learn that Joseph was called to his father's side because Jacob was near death. Joseph took along his two sons, Manasseh and Ephraim. When Jacob heard that Joseph had arrived, he "rallied his strength and sat up on the bed" (Genesis 48:2). At this meeting, Jacob revealed that Joseph would receive a double inheritance—fitting since he had rescued his family during a famine. The other brothers would each receive a share, then Joseph would have two, one for each son. When the twelve tribes of Israel are listed, we always see the names of these two sons of Joseph, each of them founding a tribe.

Jacob blessed Joseph and the two grandsons in the traditional way. He laid his hands on them. As he blessed Joseph, he said:

May the God before whom my fathers
Abraham and Isaac walked faithfully,
the God who has been my shepherd
all my life to this day,
the Angel who has delivered me from all harm
—may he bless these boys.
May they be called by my name
and the names of my fathers Abraham and Isaac,
and may they increase greatly upon the earth.

—Genesis 48:15–16

One way to age graciously is to bless our children and our grandchildren. Gary Smalley and John Trent wrote a wonderful book on that subject a number of years ago, simply called *The Blessing*. It's so important that we pray both for and with those who succeed us on this planet. It's meaningful to do it on a special occasion, as Jacob did, and also to do it more generally, finding opportunities for blessings.

My wife was a great devotee of this book, and as each of our seven grandchildren was born, she suggested they be brought to our home for a blessing. By the way, both sets of grandparents were there, and I think this made the events even more meaningful. Both grandfathers laid hands on the infants and, in the presence of the entire family, prayed and blessed the children.

I'm sure some would find such a thing peculiar in our modern culture. But in the ancient world it was a powerful tradition, and it has no less power today. As the children grow older, they see the photographs or home movies of their blessing. They hear about the whole family coming together to affirm God's presence in their lives. That's highly meaningful symbolism to children, and it's a terrific way to show our love and encouragement, too.

It's interesting that just as Jacob had received the blessing of Isaac, rather than his older brother Esau, he now gave his blessing to the younger son, Ephraim, rather than Manasseh, who was the eldest. Remember, in those times, the older son was the heir, and he was the one who was blessed. Sometimes life comes full circle. God was working out his will for both sons, rather than just one, to be the founding fathers of their tribes.

It's also worth noting that Jacob's family brought their spiritual heritage to a pagan environment. Joseph no doubt wore Egyptian garb and followed the local fashions. He spoke the language—but he didn't compromise his faith in any way. He never followed after Egyptian gods, and so effective was he in his work that people gave him no problems about his faith. When we work with excellence, it's amazing how much more tolerant our culture will be.

> **IN THE** back of our mind, we're wondering about our own final acts. How much more time? Who will mourn us?

I have a son who is a police sergeant, and one who is a pastor. Both call me and ask me to pray for them. I see that in so many ways, it still means something to them, in adulthood, to receive my blessing. We never stop yearning for the love and approval of our parents, and we never stop feeling the strength of parental encouragement.

So we can't let the time get away from us: Parents, children, and grandparents need to express their love and approval to each other. Our parents have blessed us, and as both of us grow older, we can begin to bless them.

MOURNING GLORY

Another quality of aging grace is a healthy approach to the reality of death. As we all know, growing old means becoming well acquainted with the obituary page. In earlier years, we attended a lot of weddings; then we went to baby showers. Now we find ourselves at funerals of people we've known and loved. In the back of our mind, we're wondering about our own final acts. How much more time? Who will mourn us? It's a spiritual and an emotional challenge to have a healthy and positive approach to the reality of death.

When Jacob died, we find Joseph mourning him with genuine emotion (Genesis 50:1). As a younger man, I always came to this passage and wondered about Joseph weeping over someone who was so elderly, whose time had clearly come. Now, having lost both parents, I understand. My sister Roseanne and I used to tell each other that it would be a blessing for Mom when she passed away; she'd be with the Lord; it would be "for the best," spiritually. But when the news came that my mother was gone, I wept deeply.

Grief is real and healthy. Our minds tell us that death is natural, that those we love are in a better place; but as Pascal said, the heart has its reasons which reason doesn't know. We've lost someone for now. We can't see them, hug them, tell them of our love.

The Bible tells us there is "a time to weep and a time to laugh, a time to mourn and a time to dance" (Ecclesiastes 3:44). Jesus himself wept at the loss of his friend Lazarus, even knowing he would see his friend again—and quite soon, at that. But the Bible also tells us we "do not grieve like the rest of mankind, who have no hope" (1 Thessalonians 4:13).

This is a matter for which we need to let our faith transform us. Do we really believe that the next life is vastly superior to this one? Do we really believe we'll be reunited, this time without the sins and imperfections of earthly life? If so, that should have an impact on how we look at death. Our farewells should be grounded in hope, not despair. The heart is broken, and we mourn. But we are transformed by the renewing of our minds, and in time our grief should take flight as hope and quiet joy.

The truth of heaven should also impact our feelings of urgency in sharing the gospel with those we love. Have we done everything possible to share the reason for our hope with those we love, and with everyone else, for that matter? I know where I'm going after this life is over, and I don't want to leave behind anyone I care about.

As we age gracefully, we don't deny the reality of death. We embrace it as a natural transition. We feel as Paul did when he said, "For to me, to live is Christ and to die is gain" (Philippians 1:21). There he sat in imprisonment, his eyesight leaving him, health problems cascading, and he regarded himself in a win/win scenario. No mere physical prison could keep him down; nobody could poison his attitude. Others would have seen prison vs. beheading as a lose/lose scenario, but Jesus is the ultimate, all-victorious difference. Not even the trial of aging can suppress the joy that he gives us.

One final point about Joseph and the loss of his father: He took great pains to give his father the burial he had requested. Jacob didn't want Egypt to be his final resting place. He had an abiding love for his home country, and he had secured Joseph's promise to bury him there. In that day, it was no convenient matter to carry through with such a promise. Joseph had to secure special permission and lead a large expedition to Canaan. What do we have to learn here? In these times, we are in denial about death because this culture doesn't really believe there is anything beyond this life. So we rush through funerals. We make quick appearances at the funeral home, take a casserole to the family, and breathe a sigh of relief when it's past us.

But funerals and memorial services should be times of closure with a foundation of worship. They can be extremely meaningful. They can bring people to Christ. They can tighten family bonds. Over the years, I've seen time and again that funeral events can be among the most spiritually positive events we have.

When my father passed on, the weather was beyond terrible: a snowstorm with near-blizzard conditions on the day of his funeral. The funeral director suggested closing the service and having a private burial; he promised to take Dad to the cemetery himself. I had to concede the practicality of that, but it was important to me to be at the grave for the burial. My brother and I, along with our sons, followed the hearse in a four-wheel-drive vehicle and plowed through the snow into the cemetery.

The two gravediggers were shivering, huddled beside the grave. As we turned to leave, I led a prayer that was emotionally difficult to deliver, thanking God that my father was now in the loving arms of his Lord. The event was poignant, unforgettable to those of us there. As we walked away, I felt the biting cold, looked at the layered snow, and thought about how it must feel to bury someone without an eternal hope—winter with no prospect of spring.

I couldn't imagine living like that, in a permanent, chilly wasteland of despair. Instead, our faith in heaven was light and warmth enough to cut through the most vicious storm. We were cold in the body, but our hearts were kindled by a fire that could never be doused.

DEBT-FREE

The first book of the Bible closes with the death of one of the great patriarchs. Joseph grows old, dies, and is himself buried. Let's examine one final lesson from his life, one final thing that he got exactly right before he left this world.

We're told that his brothers had a lingering fear that he hadn't really forgiven them. They said, "What if Joseph holds a grudge against us and pays us back for all the wrongs we did to him?" (Genesis 50:15). Maybe he was waiting for Jacob to die. Remember, this was a pre-Christian world, and grace was not the norm. We could say it still isn't.

For those who walk with God, as Joseph did, forgiveness is profound and complete. These people live in the present, and the past is dead. Joseph had already told his brothers that what they meant for evil, God meant for good. Joseph meant it, too.

We can turn this one around and ask what the brothers—also

aging—revealed about themselves through their doubts. Had they for-given themselves?

Christians, of all people, shouldn't be plagued by emotional debt, whether directed at self or others. Paul writes, "Let no debt remain out-standing, except the continuing debt to love one another" (Romans 13:8). When the Son sets us free, we are truly free. Aging gracefully means being liberated from regret, knowing that God is in control and has been all along.

CLOSER TO HEAVEN

Finally, we notice that Joseph never forgot God. This is highly signifi-cant, because this is a man who spent most of his life in a pagan culture. How easy it would have been to "go native" in Egypt, taking on the local gods and beliefs just as he did the local language and fashions. He remembered and worshiped his Lord and God.

Surprisingly, we find only one mention of Joseph in the New Testament. In the famous "roll call of faith," where Old Testament heroes are celebrated, it says this: "By faith Joseph, when his end was near, spoke about the exodus of the Israelites from Egypt and gave instructions concerning the burial of his bones" (Hebrews 11:22). God had uprooted him and planted him in Egypt, and there he had bloomed. He knew that while Egypt had been his destiny, Canaan was God's plan for his descendants.

It's significant that he ended his life talking about the future rather than reflecting upon the past. It's a mark of wisdom, of a faith that God is doing something much wider and deeper than our short lives. It is said that the sign of true perspective is when, as old people, we can plant trees to bloom long after we're gone. Joseph planted seeds that bloomed into a great and powerful nation.

As we grow older, we draw closer to heaven, and people should be able to see it begin to glow from our countenance. We shouldn't be sad, shriveling creatures consumed by regret and obsessed with the past, but more like children once again, thrilled that the ultimate Christmas morning lies just around the corner.

No, aging isn't particularly fun. It is a time marked by losses of various kinds. We grieve for the vitality of youth we've lost. We grieve for the friends and family who are taken from our midst. But we grieve not as those who have no hope. Deep within us lies the certainty that it's often darkest just before the dawn, and this will be a dawn like no other. Jesus said, "I am the resurrection and the life. The one who believes in me will live, even though they die" (John 11:25).

GOD IS WORKING

At the beginning of the chapter, I hinted that there was more to the story of my mother, after Alzheimer's began to pull her away from us. It had been such a sad experience, watching her lose even her recognition of who I was. I began to feel that she was already gone.

On my next-to-last visit, my mother and I simply didn't connect. I sat for a while before finally taking her hand and saying, "Mom, I'm going to leave now, but first I'd like to read Psalm 23 to you." And then something happened. As I read the words, life came back into her eyes, if briefly. She began to quote the words with me.

The disease was strong, but my mother was still there, and whatever vital memories had drained away from her, she still held the Shepherd Psalm close. In the valley of the shadow, her Lord was with her. It's hard to express how much comfort I felt. I left with a lighter heart that week, reflecting on the fact that at any time, God is at work in ways we never see. I thanked him and praised him on my way home.

There was one more visit. Naturally I read the 23rd Psalm again, hoping to see that same light in my mother's eyes. But this time, there was no response; she simply stared into space. My brother was with me, and he said, "Mom, do you remember your favorite hymn? It was

'There Is a Fountain Filled with Blood.' Why don't we sing that one?" And as my brother and I began to sing, it happened again—the inspired melody brought my mother back to us. She followed along with us, both singing and humming.

To be honest, I was almost too moved to make music. I thought,

Thank you, Lord. Thank you for reminding me. Music is one of the most precious of your gifts, the way it touches us with the beauty of heaven deep inside. Thank you for caring for our mother.

We ask why aging is so difficult. We want to know why God would allow something like Alzheimer's. Again I conclude that every act of God carries more meaning than our minds can grasp. No matter how we mourn, no matter how sad some days can be, we must believe that God is loving and good, and that someday, in his presence, we'll see the whole picture and understand that the darkest moments of this life were necessary ingredients to the brightest miracles he was planning.

Someday, my mother and I will talk about that together. And I suspect that once again, we'll share the 23rd Psalm and sing the praises of our God. And the memories of aging will make us smile, because we will be far beyond its earthly clutches.

We'll be citizens of eternity, partakers of unbroken joy.

QUESTIONS FOR YOU

1. What attitudes about aging can be found in your family? What about you?

2. What factors make aging one of life's most difficult obstacles? What are some of its advantages?

3. What are some ways that parents and grandparents can bless their children?

4. What are some ways that believers can avoid bitterness and regret as they age?

5. What can you be doing in life right now to create more satisfaction when you look back later?

12: FINAL ACT

IT WAS THE FIRST Great Moment of my life—from the perspective of a six-year-old boy, a momentous occasion.

It was Children's Day at church. Yes, there used to be such a thing. Mother's Day, Father's Day, Children's Day. Eventually somebody figured out that "*every* day is children's day," just as we tell our kids today; or perhaps Hallmark couldn't make enough profit on the concept.

But it was indeed Children's Day, and it was my shining hour at the age of six. I stood before the congregation and proudly repeated the first ten verses of John 14. I felt like a star as I received the praise and affirmation of a world of grownups.

After the service, our elderly preacher, D. P. Shaffer, asked my mother, "Is this the boy who quoted the Scripture today?" My mother seemed to glow with pride, and the sight of her face did the same for me. Brother Shaffer placed his palsied hand on my shoulder and said, "Young man, you sure would make a good preacher someday."

For me, it was what we know in Christianity as a *calling* moment. His words had the ring of destiny, of rich purpose. I felt the grand idea sink into my heart and soul. Surely this was true; surely the boy who quoted ten gospel verses was destined to stand behind a pulpit someday and share the gospel. I clung to that intention as a child.

But childhood did not cling to me; I passed on into the confusing world of adolescence, when ideas of self and the world are revisited and revamped. I didn't forget how the great old man had placed his hand upon my shoulder, but the power of the memory was fading fast. For one thing, I hated the idea of speaking in public. Nor did I love the idea of church attendance as I had in childhood. As a brooding teen, I attended strictly from obligation.

New dreams had displaced the old—dreams that nearly always had to do with the world of sports. My high school basketball team was a very strong one, and its goal was so simple and powerful: win the state tournament. We were galvanized by the lure of it, and my daydreams took that shape.

I really believed my dream would unfold like a fairy tale, and at the best of times: my senior year. We won our league championship surely enough, and we entered the state tournament as favorites. We set our sights on that trophy as our destiny. But after leading one of our opponents by 14 in the final quarter, everything came apart. Our shots rimmed out; our defense caved in. Suddenly we were the bit players in someone else's fairy tale, as our opponents hit a shot at the buzzer to send the game into overtime. They cheered and celebrated as we walked back to the bench, faces downcast. The other team rode the surge of momentum to victory, and we were crushed.

There I was at seventeen years old, and it felt as if there would never be a Christmas morning again, never a spring day. I had built my whole world around a prize that was snatched away at the last minute and would never come again. High school was over. The players would go their separate ways.

Seeing me sink into depression, my older sister Rosanne invited me to visit her for five days at Cincinnati Bible College, "just to get away," as she put it with gentle persuasion. I could stay in the men's dorm with some of her friends. What a loving gift from a big sister.

The guys at the college took me in, befriended me, encouraged me. At times I forgot I was supposed to be crestfallen, and found myself laughing. At the end of the visit, I thought, "What a bunch of great guys! If I wanted to be a minister, this is where I'd go."

But I didn't want to be a minister; I wanted to go to Clarion College in Pennsylvania and play some more basketball, chase another trophy. Such was the plan. Three weeks later, when my dad and I drove to Clarion at the coach's invitation, I was filled with fresh hope and ready to turn the page to my basketball future.

What a disappointment when the coach sent word that, due to an unexpected development, he couldn't be there to meet us. An assistant coach subbed for him, and he listlessly pointed out this building and that, telling us to take our own tour. I hated the tiny gym; I couldn't imagine any truly great college basketball being played in it.

Meanwhile, I saw some of the students partying—something I hadn't even thought about. I began to have doubts that had nothing to do with athletics. While I didn't really want to be a preacher, I did want to be a Christian, as I'd been raised; and I wasn't sure where the temptations of a secular campus environment would lead me.

The drive home was quiet. I thought about the unexpectedly great visit to the Bible college and the unexpectedly poor one to the "basketball college." In my reflections, I felt the hand of D. P. Shaffer on my shoulder; I heard his warm voice suggesting a godly future. Prophecy or presumption? What had I learned about myself in the two trips?

My father was jolted when I suddenly emerged from my trance, blurting out, "Dad, I'm not going to Clarion! God wants me to go to Cincinnati and study for the ministry." At that moment, it was as if every mist of confusion suddenly burned away from the bright sunlight of divine calling. It was so clear. As we reached home and quickly told my mother the news, she wept for joy.

And yet there was something strange about the whole thing. I knew I hadn't made all the right choices through high school. I had failed to make Christ the first priority in my life, and I wasn't sure where I stood with God these days. Yet here was my calling, so powerful.

I had walked a very strange road between the age of six and this moment, and yet God was willing to embrace me and point me forward, as if I had never left his side. As a matter of fact, I could see how he had used every part of my journey to bring me to this moment—the passion and teamwork of sports, the discipline of reaching for a goal, and particularly the lessons learned from upside-down priorities. My new sense of purpose was stronger because I'd had to struggle to arrive at it. And I understood what it meant to pursue eternal rewards, because I'd had some experience with pursuing earthly, temporary ones.

God had nothing to do with any poor choices I made. But he had everything to do with the education I received from them. As with Joseph, he intended it all for good.

THE PARADOX OF JOSEPH

It's not as if Joseph and I had too much in common, however. At least not as I saw it. Like you, I would read his story and think: This was a man of legend—a hero, an ancient champion! Who today has a story like that? I took so many wrong turns, but once Joseph got started, he followed God with near-perfect obedience.

Unique among biblical heroes—except, of course, for Jesus—Joseph ran an outstanding race, leaped gracefully over every hurdle, and finished strong. We'd be tempted to call his character unbelievable if the book of Genesis wasn't a history. And a history it is. Joseph just happens to shine so brightly, even in a hall of champions that includes people like Moses, David, and Abraham.

Yes, he was outstanding in his achievements, but here's the paradox. The tests and trials he faced, once you truly examine them, are no different than those *we* face. Sure, you may not have been sold into physical bondage, but you've surely been the object of jealousy. You might, for example, have been at the center of terrible conflict in your family. You might be one of the countless people today who is a child or a veteran of a broken home.

And while you may not have been sent to prison on a false accusation, you've probably been unjustly treated by petty individuals somewhere along the line. Our world is a crowded one, a desperate one, and it has no shortage of characters who lack character—people more than willing to lie to you or about you, just to claim some small advantage.

While you may never have been promoted straight from prison to the seat of international power, you've been given your own opportunity by God. And while it may not seem to be world-changing, you can never know the ripples your contribution might send out. You can never see, in this life, how many people will be affected by your simple obedience to God and his principles.

You have your own chance to shine, just as Joseph did. You have your time to bloom in a place you never expected to be planted. It may not be on the harsh desert sands of Egypt, but it could be in the hustle and bustle of the marketplace; the sacred responsibilities of a family; the multitude of needs in your community.

Languages, cultures, fashions, and technology change, but human nature never does. Every temptation Joseph faced, every question he asked before the heavens, every opportunity God bestowed upon him—all of these are timeless and unchanging. This is why the Bible speaks to us today, and never stops being more contemporary than today's Internet newsfeed.

The other side of the equation is that if the trials of people never change, neither do the acts of God. He was at work in every moment of Joseph's story. At the time, his ways were impossible to fathom—just as they are **WHAT** questions are you now facing, and how well are you responding in patient trust and obedient action, as Joseph did? for us—and Joseph must have asked the same questions we do. Why should he be a slave? Why should prison be his reward for making the correct moral choice? Why should he spend so much time locked up?

God had a plan all along, and he was given glory and honor as the acts of men were caught up in the more comprehensive acts of God. I know I can see the acts of God in my life, right through the worst of my errors. No matter what wrong turn I might take, he knew how to point it back toward the destination he planned for me—not only that, but he made my wayward path pay off; he used everything along it to make me the servant he needed me to be.

I wonder about his acts in your life. What questions are you now facing, and how well are you responding in patient trust and obedient action, as Joseph did? Can you see the pattern of tests and trial that carry you down the road from youth and immaturity to a divine destiny?

Think in particular about the twisting paths of your own life. How has God used the tough moments, the moments that felt like failure at the time? What did you learn? How were you prepared for divine service?

HIS ACTS AND YOUR CHOICES

Two roads diverged in a yellow wood—profound poetry by Robert Frost.

That visit to two colleges was a moment in which I stood at the signpost myself. Two possible futures opened themselves to me, and I had a choice to make. I know that God helped me make that choice, but he left it to me. He would never violate our free will, because it is that very will that builds the strength of character he desires in us.

I chose my path and walked down it for years, until I came to another crossroad. "We've started a new church in Louisville, Kentucky," said my friend Butch Dabney one day as he came to visit me. "It has terrific potential."

I listened as he talked to me about this new startup, Southeast Christian Church, and I felt his passion and certainty that God was going to do something special. He was describing a new work that called out to me; I envied the adventure on which he and those Kentucky people were about to embark. Then he said, "We feel a strong sense that the Lord wants us to call a preacher who can come in as a young man and grow with us." And of course I understood where this conversation was heading.

I was twenty-two, and it was precisely the kind of opportunity that appealed to me—that would appeal to any young preacher, I'm sure. These Louisville folks were going to do something powerful and inspiring for the kingdom of God, and I wanted to be a part of it.

There was one problem. I'd made a promise to the Monterey Christian Church, where I was currently preaching. I would be their first full-time minister in a hundred years, and they were conscious of what that meant to their history and their dreams. Therefore they had asked for a commitment that I stay the course for at least one year.

That had been five months ago.

The more I thought it through, the more I realized my way was clear. I could have rationalized my emotions and convinced myself that God was calling me to a new work, and that he would provide for Monterey some other way. Except that wasn't the God we know from Scripture. That wasn't the God who keeps all his promises and commands us to do the same.

I thanked Butch Dabney, told him I knew God was about to do terrific things in Louisville, and explained that I was bound to a sacred commitment to my present congregation. And I figured that would be the last I would hear from Butch, at least on this particular subject.

Three months later, however, it was Butch on the phone again. "Bob," he said, "we still haven't found a preacher." Given the opportunity that the new Southeast Christian Church offered, I couldn't help but be surprised. "Two members of our pulpit committee drove up to hear you preach this morning," he continued. "We continue to have a strong feeling about you, and we admire the fact that you honor your word. We want to honor that, too. So consider this. We'd like you to come and visit with us. Your commitment binds you to a hundred more days or so at your current church, and we're willing to wait. Will you come, see our work, and pray with our elders?"

I did that. And four months later, I began a path that I followed for forty years in Louisville, where God did immeasurably more than all I could ask or imagine. I often wonder how things might have been different if I had gone on my own initiative, rather than in obedience to God and my own integrity. For me, the lesson is that we must trust and obey, waiting upon him, sensitive to his timing. And we have to make the right choices, just as Joseph did.

God makes the plans and you make the choices. Your decisions will determine how well your life harmonizes with his great blueprint. And don't worry: You're likely to make a few missteps. Joseph wasn't perfect either, and we can be sure that he had a bad day every now and then; there simply wasn't space to record it. But when you're obedient—when you keep in step with the Spirit (Galatians 5:25)—there's no limit to the miracles he will do.

ON TO PLAN B

In a lifetime of observation, I've noticed that among the greatest of the acts of God are those that come in the aftermath of our failures. His mercy never ends. God had a plan for Jacob, who had received his birthright through cheating, and who had turned out to be a flawed father. God had a plan for a group of brothers who were, at one point, intent on murder before settling for a lesser evil. God always has a master plan, and yet it always allows for our humanity. It's the size of your potential as well as your shortcomings.

You could present most of the great narrative of the Bible as a story of the failure of people and the faithfulness of God; the stubborn waywardness of humanity and the perfect way of God. Consider the story of Moses. We know that God had his hand upon Moses' shoulder from the very beginning, when he was spared by the wrath of a Pharaoh by being placed in a basket, only to be found by the royal family. God, who knows all things, surely whispered in the baby's ear,

"You'll make a great shepherd for Me someday."

He meant for Moses to be a shepherd of a nation, and yet Moses became a shepherd of sheep. This happened because, in a fit of temper, he killed an Egyptian man who was persecuting a Jew. Moses, who was being raised in privilege as a prince, had blown it. He had to vanish into the wilderness to care for livestock and brood about what might have been. And yet God didn't abandon him. He used the failure of Moses, and the quiet of the desert, to rebuild the true shepherd he desired.

What God asks from us is a "long obedience in the same direction," in the memorable phrase of Eugene Peterson. What we give him is fitful obedience with a lack of direction. Yet all the while, God is allowing us to go places that he knows he can use to mold us. By the way, the Bible continues this same theme in the story of Moses leading the children of Israel to the Promised Land. The shortest distance between two points is a straight line, which would have been a short walk of a few weeks in this case. But the people wandered for forty years because of their lack of faith—and still God got them to the land of promise.

So with the many lessons we can take from Joseph, one is *not* this: that God can use us only if we make every right move. God is patient, forgiving, and always ready to walk with us to our Plan B, which turns out to fit right into his Plan A. Your decisions count, and your disobedience will carry consequences. But it will never bring you outside the reach of your heavenly Father who loves you, who is eternally patient and eternally loving, and whose most cherished act is the act of your redemption. For him, the final act is the one best depicted when a prodigal son runs into his father's embrace, and is bathed by tears of forgiveness and love.

ACROSS YOUR HORIZON

Finally, my friend, remember that this life is lived out on a tiny grain of a planet called Earth, in a brief moment of time, all of which is part of a vast picture far beyond our comprehension. Think of the irony: Joseph, his hands chained together, made the long walk to Egypt, and surely felt utterly alone, utterly insignificant, completely forgotten by God.

Yet pull back the camera and get a slightly larger view. It was a moment in Joseph's life that would lead him from Canaan to a prison, and then to a position of high responsibility. That knowledge alone, a simple matter of his future timeline, would have encouraged Joseph's heart. He simply had to move on without that understanding, because there was character to be built, faith to be sharpened in the laboratory of life.

But pull back the camera even farther, and the surprises mount. As Joseph walked to a foreign and frightening land in those chains, the history of his nation was altered seismically. The time would come when his family would follow him there. They would multiply, become the people known as the Israelites, and fall into bondage. Then God would raise up Moses to lead them home again. Just as God was doing something in the life of Joseph, he was also active in forming the character of his chosen people.

Then, pull back the camera once again—pulling it back over centuries this time. God was doing something through that nation as part of his plan for all of humanity. From the line of these people would come Jesus—God entering into history in the flesh to save us from our sins. The story of Joseph is filled with foreshadowing, "pre-echoes" of Jesus Christ, the Son of God. For instance, Joseph was betrayed and put into a dark pit, then ascended and saved Egypt. Jesus was betrayed and descended into the dark pit of death, then rose to go and save the world. Joseph brought his brothers to Egypt, where they became a great nation; Jesus founded the church upon his eleven disciples, and they became a great nation. Joseph provided bread for life. Jesus was the bread of life.

IF GOD sent Joseph, He is sending *you*.

God is always doing something new, but there are also beautiful, recurring patterns in his work. In everything, he is trying to reach out to people, to restore them to himself, to save them. If Joseph saved his generation from physical hunger, Jesus came to answer the world's spiritual hunger. If God sent Joseph, he is sending *you*.

As you have read these words, what words has God been whispering into your ear? Which of the trials of Joseph spoke most urgently to your heart? Which acts of God have you considered most deeply? Surely you've picked up this volume because God is working again, reaching out to use you in some redemptive adventure. Have you decided what it is? How will you respond?

It's a long walk from Canaan, to Egypt, and back again. And a lot of things can happen in that journey. As you make your own pilgrimage, however it might be defined, my prayer is that you'll never forget that God is with you, each step of the way; that your questions about his ways, as you struggle with them, will increase your faith and draw you closer to his presence; and that, at the end of the road, you find the joyful and fulfilling destiny that he has mapped out for you all along.

May the peace of God go with you as you follow the steps of Joseph—and of Jesus himself.

QUESTIONS FOR YOU

1. Describe a "crossroads moment" from your own life. In retrospect, how was God at work? How did he use that moment?

2. As you complete this study, what issues in your own life have been reflected most in these chapters? Why?

3. What part of Joseph's life did you find most relevant to your own experience? Why?

4. Explain this statement from the text: "We often turn to Plan B, and discover it fits beautifully into God's Plan A."

5. If you were to make one change in your life based upon this study, what would it be? Any reason you can't make that change?

NOTES

1. Jerry Sittser, *A Grace Disguised: How the Soul Grows through Loss* (Grand Rapids, MI: Zondervan, 2005), 42.

2. Paul Koring, "Parents: do you know where your teens are online? Probably not, study says," The Globe and Mail, June 28, 2012, accessed April 1, 2013. www.theglobeandmail.com/news/world/worldview/parents-do-you-know-where-your-teens-are-online-probably-not-study-says/article4376192/.

3. Rob Rienow, *When They Turn Away* (Grand Rapids, MI: Kregel, 2010), 103.

4. Jim Murphy, *Inner Excellence* (New York: McGraw Hill, 2009), 80–81.

5. Thomas Wilson quoted in CBS News, "Iraq-Bound GIs Grill Rumsfeld," *CBS News*, February 11, 2009, accessed April 16, 2013. www.cbsnews.com/2100-500257_162-659990.html.

6. Michael P. Ghiglieri and Thomas M. Myers, *Over the Edge: Death in Grand Canyon: Gripping Accounts of All Known Fatal Mishaps in the Most Famous of the World's Seven Natural Wonders* (Flagstaff, AZ: Puma, 2012).

7. Eric Metaxas, *Bonhoeffer: Pastor, Martyr, Prophet, Spy* (Nashville, TN: Thomas Nelson, 2011), 514.

8. Ibid., 515.

9. Julia Cameron, ed., *Christ Our Reconciler* (Downers Grove, IL: InterVarsity Press, 2012), 200–201.

10. Centers for Disease Control and Prevention, "An Estimated 1 in 10 U.S. Adults Report Depression," March 31, 2011, accessed April 26, 2013. www.cdc.gov/features/dsdepression/.

11. Bob Reccord, *Forged by Fire* (Nashville, TN: B&H Publishing, 2000), 156.

12. Cameron, 201.

ACKNOWLEDGMENTS

I AM DEEPLY GRATEFUL to many who have assisted in writing this book. Thanks to my son Phil, and Shane Sooter, director of City on a Hill.

I'm thankful for City on a Hill Productions who encouraged me to do video instruction for the movie *Acts of God*, which served as the inspiration for writing this book.

Thanks also to Pat McIntyre and Debbie Carper for editing assistance. I'm especially grateful to Rob Suggs for his invaluable contribution in helping to prepare the manuscript for publication.

I also want to thank Moody Publishers for their involvement and endorsement of this effort.

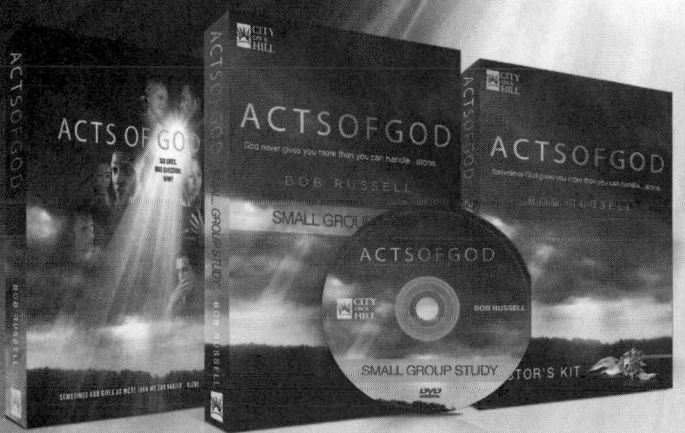

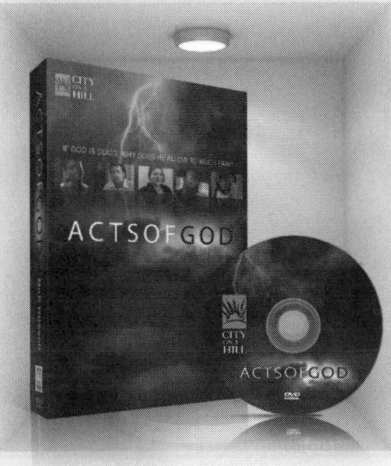

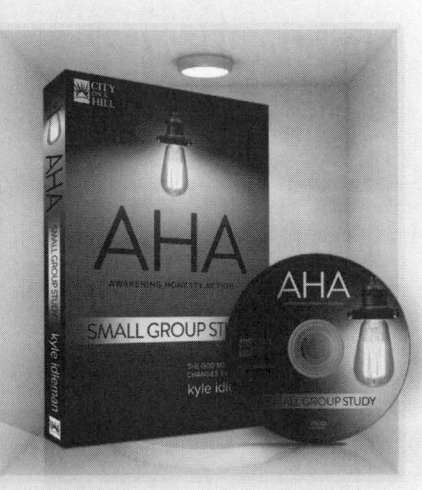

CITY
ON A
HILL

THE SONG

An aspiring
singer-songwriter's
life and marriage suffer
when the song he writes
for his wife propels
him to stardom.
Based on the life
and writings of
King Solomon.

COMING FALL 2014
TheSongFilm.com